"THIS IS FEEDBAG ONE. STAND BY, I'LL GET HIM!"

I got a good Sidewinder growl with about five Gs on the airplane and a look-down of about 30 degrees.

The AIM-9 tried hard. It almost made the turn. Flying outside the MiG's tilted starboard wingtip, the 'winder exploded but inflicted no visible damage.

Then the MiG driver made a fundamental—and fatal—error. He reversed his turn from port to starboard, lighting his afterburner as he rolled wings-level. I fell directly in trail at one mile, one G, and fired my second Sidewinder. It was a direct hit, right up the tailpipe. But the MiG was still flying in one piece.

I was closing quickly. I popped the speed brakes to avoid an overshoot and acquired a decent sight picture. With the pipper on top of the MiG I fired 167 rounds. The airplane was raked from fore to aft across the top and came apart.

Kocar saw the 17 fall and exclaimed, "Way to go, Feedbag!" Thirty-five seconds had passed.

Other Bantam Books by Barrett Tillman
WARRIORS

ON YANKEE STATION

The Naval Air War Over Vietnam

CDR. JOHN B. NICHOLS, USN (Ret.)
and
BARRETT TILLMAN

™
FALCON

BANTAM BOOKS

NEW YORK • TORONTO • LONDON • SYDNEY • AUCKLAND

This edition contains the complete text
of the original hardcover edition.
NOT ONE WORD HAS BEEN OMITTED.

ON YANKEE STATION
A Bantam Falcon Book / published by arrangement with
Naval Institute Press

PRINTING HISTORY
Naval Institute Press edition published July 1987
Bantam edition / July 1988
Bantam reissue / October 1991

ISBN 0-553-27216-0

Published simultaneously in the United States and Canada

Bantam Books are published by Bantam Books, a division of
Bantam Doubleday Dell Publishing Group, Inc. Its trademark,
consisting of the words "Bantam Books" and the portrayal of a
rooster, is Registered in U.S. Patent and Trademark Office and in
other countries. Marca Registrada. Bantam Books, 666 Fifth Ave-
nue, New York, New York 10103.

PRINTED IN THE UNITED STATES OF AMERICA

OPM   0 9 8 7 6 5

*To those Missing in Action
and to their families*

In Vietnam we tried and failed in a just cause.
"No more Vietnams" *can* mean we will not try again.
It *should* mean we will not fail again.

—RICHARD M. NIXON
1985

CONTENTS

Douglas A-4 Skyhawk

FOREWORD

As a former A-4 pilot and twenty-two-year veteran of the navy, I have a deep interest in the subjects addressed in *On Yankee Station*. In this book the authors provide a perspective on the rules of engagement that guided the naval air war over Vietnam.

Despite the complexity of the subject, Commander John B. Nichols and Barrett Tillman offer a vivid and thorough account. Drawing upon his experience as a four-tour WestPac F-8 pilot, Commander Nichols highlights the personal involvement of naval aviators in a very frustrating war. Analyzing the role of naval aviation, the authors provide an accurate assessment of its importance to our efforts during that conflict.

The striking descriptions of tangles with MiGs make this book exciting reading to those involved in the air war. Of equal interest to students of military history are the sections describing the deadly threat of antiaircraft guns and surface-to-air missiles. Having been shot down by a SAM, I can fully appreciate the difficulties they posed to pilots already constricted by bureaucratic and political decision makers.

On Yankee Station: The Naval Air War Over Vietnam is an important study for its technological and historical perspective. It will provide invaluable reading for all concerned with the role of naval aviation, both during the Vietnam War and in our nation's future.

JOHN MCCAIN
U.S. Senator

INTRODUCTION

The Vietnam War—more properly considered as the Second Indochina War—was conducted by Americans under a set of orders collectively known as the rules of engagement (ROE). It was not the first, nor would it be the last, time the United States imposed such regulations upon its armed forces. The Vietnam ROE, however, differed from those of earlier conflicts in one important way. Each type of force (for example, carrier- and land-based aviation, infantry, and riverine forces) received its own individualized set of rules that contained detailed instructions as to what tactics could and could not be employed. The term that described the level of involvement of nonmilitary decision makers in military matters was "micromanagement."

This volume is not a detailed study of navy air's rules of engagement. Such a work could not be done now because of security restrictions and incomplete data. Rather, what follows is part memoir, part analysis. It's a cockpit view of the carrier air war over North Vietnam—with benefit of hindsight.

Veteran Vietnam aviators will find much in these pages that is familiar to them. Having "been there" at some point between 1965 and 1973, they know the effect of ROE at the tactical level. They know also the fallacy of the belief that airpower "failed" in Vietnam.

They know instinctively what this book will examine consciously: that airpower was misunderstood and misapplied throughout Southeast Asia for seven years or more, and that when aviation was applied correctly, it achieved results.

Two reasons insist upon a treatment of this subject, one historical and one operational. Both reasons are of interest to today's youngsters—some still in school, some in cockpits—who one day might benefit from the information in these pages.

First, documentation of practices at the tactical level is limited. Because of the press of time during the war and now because of the passage of time, there is a gap in the knowledge available to those who themselves might someday have to fly in battle. Vietnam veterans have been surprised to learn that college courses are being taught about the Indochina wars. Young adults in 1986 have little memory of the war years. Some are no more familiar with the Tonkin Gulf Resolution than with the Monroe Doctrine. For some, the names of Tet and Ia Drang are no more meaningful than Shiloh or Belleau Wood. We can at least preserve the memory— the emotions and the sensations—of how it felt to be there. We hope in this book to impart a sense of what it was like to fly from Yankee Station between 1964 and 1973.

Second, we hope that young warriors may profit from the knowledge and experience of old warriors. Fewer than 10 percent of the naval aviators flying today logged a mission in Vietnam. By recalling the details of missions, perhaps we can contribute to the "institutional memory," add to the data bank of experience a young aviator can draw on in time of trouble.

Although aircraft, weapons, and techniques have changed in the years since the Vietnam War, the fundamentals remain constant. Men still fight less because of cause or country and more because they seek to be worthy of the esteem of their comrades. Vietnam vets, whether they humped an M-16 through the Delta or rolled in on Thanh Hoa Bridge in an A-4, understand this. Government leaders and policy makers need to relearn that fact. The lessons are available for the taking, for there will always be flak and SAMs and MiGs. And there will always be rules of engagement.

CDR. JOHN B. NICHOLS, USN (RET.)
BARRETT TILLMAN

ON YANKEE STATION

U.S.S. Langley

BACKGROUND TO DOCTRINE

The Secretary of the Navy has decided that the science of aerial navigation has reached that point where aircraft must form a large part of our naval force.

> —*Navy Department news release*
> *10 January 1914*

By the time of the Tonkin Gulf Incident in August 1964, the U.S. Navy had many decades of aviation experience. The carriers *Ticonderoga* (CVA-14) and *Constellation* (CVA-64) that launched the retaliatory strikes against North Vietnamese PT-boat bases were directly descended from the USS *Langley* (CV-1), converted from a collier in 1922. The supersonic jets launched by the *Ticonderoga* and the *Constellation* were a far cry from the flying machines that the first generation of tailhook aviators nursed into the air from the *Langley*'s improvised flight deck.

A half-century of institutional experience had brought U.S. Naval Aviation to a position of leadership in that esoteric martial art. Combat operations in World War II and Korea, combined with a growing number of experienced naval airmen able to articulate, consolidate, and pass on their knowledge, proved beyond doubt that in the latter part of the twentieth century seapower was impossible without airpower.

By 1964, although at least nine nations operated fixed-winged aircraft carriers, the United States possessed more flattops that the rest of the world's navies combined. With sixteen strike carriers and ten antisubmarine carriers, the U.S. Navy as able to deploy one or more flattops almost anywhere in the world.

Not all these carriers, of course, were available at any one time. A new generation of ships emerged with the commissioning of the *Forrestal* (CV-59) in 1955, but the U.S. Navy still relied heavily upon the World War II generation: the numerous *Essex*-class ships and three postwar *Midways*. The *Essexes* were long-lived and versatile. Originally designed for a standard displacement of 27,100 tons, with axial decks operating World War II aircraft, they were extensively modified during the 1950s. In the SCB-27C, that is "27-Charlie" configuration, they were modernized with angled flight decks, steam catapults, and numerous structural modifications. Capable of operating most jet aircraft in the fleet, the *Essex* ships were employed as either strike or antisubmarine platforms.

The *Forrestal* and subsequent designs were significant advances over the *Essex* ships. They displaced twice the fuel, three times the aviation fuel and two and one-half times the ordnance. More stable in heavy seas, they could operate aircraft 96 percent of the time in the roughest seas. They enjoyed better safety records than the *Essex* class.[1]

An *Essex or Forrestal* carrier usually embarked about seventy aircraft in the strike role. Around 1964, *Essex and Forrestal* ships carried different types of fighters. The F-4 Phantom, for example, flew exclusively from the larger ships, and when the A-6 Intruder bomber joined the fleet, it, too, was found only in big-deck air wings.

Regardless of ship type—*Essex*-, *Midway*-, or *Forrestal*-class—the air wing composition was similar: two fighter squadrons; two or three attack squadrons; and early-warning, photoreconnaissance, and helicopter detachments. Typically, the 27-Charlie ships flew two F-8 outfits; an A-1 and two A-4 squadrons; and RF-8s, E-1s, and KA-3 tankers. In large-deck air wings, one or both fighter squadrons had F-4s while the photoreconnaissance and the heavy attack roles were filled by A-5 Vigilantes.

Fleet air defense was the realm of the Phantom. Its interceptor configuration, with two-man crew and radar-guided missiles, was excellent for the role, day or night. But the F-4 was never intended as an air superiority fighter. Neither design nor training leaned in that direction and, as events proved, the Phantom players had to come from a long way behind to catch up with the MIGs in the Southeast Asia league.

In the Vought Crusader, the navy possessed one of the finest day fighters ever built. The F-8 community, ignoring high accident rates, perfected the doctrine and techniques of air combat maneuvering (ACM) that would make "the last gunfighter" almost invincible in combat. The F-8, though, was limited as a nightfighter, despite the variants built for that role. The small radar dish in models prior to the F-8E prevented adequate search, and ground clutter badly denigrated the low-level capability. Additionally, F-8s were not armed with radar missiles and consequently had to engage at visual distances with heat-seeking Sidewinders.

Carrier air wings were supposedly day- and night-qualified, although as noted, little nocturnal strike capability existed in the 1950s to mid-1960s. Propeller-driven Skyraiders and Skyhawk jets could bomb under flares on moonless nights, but such operations were dangerous against contemporary air defense networks. Not until the production of the next-generation carrier bomber, Grumman's superb A-6, did the fleet possess a true all-weather strike capability.

Three aircraft that served the fleet's attack squadrons were Douglas-built. The World War II-designed A-1 (née AD) Skyraider was a wonderful airplane—rugged, long-lived, and versatile. In addition to its strike role, it flew in electronic countermeasures (ECM) and airborne early-warning (AEW) variants as well. Though piston-powered and relatively slow, it possessed exceptional loiter time—a characteristic that endeared it to search-and-rescue operators. But by 1964 the age of the prop was nearing an end, and in 1968 the venerable "Spad" disappeared from the Tonkin Gulf.

Carrying the bulk of ordnance was the sporty A-4 Skyhawk. Designed by master wingsmith Ed Heinemann (as were the A-1 and A-3), this single-seater jet exemplified the designer's philosophy: simplicity, ruggedness, and ease of maintenance. The latter became extremely important as air operations intensified in 1965. Day after day, the A-4 squadrons reported 85 to 100 percent availability.[2] If one airplane kept is us in the air over North Vietnam, it was the A-4.

The big, underrated A-3 Skywarrior represented a quantum leap in size and capability of carrier aircraft when it appeared in 1956. The original design specification was for 100,000 pounds but Heinemann's Douglas team brought it in at 58,000. Intended as a nuclear bomber, the "Whale" eventually did almost everything else. It served as an ECM platform, but primarily it functioned as an aerial gas station. As one flying admiral said, "Tanker fuel is the most expensive there is. But when you need it, you need it bad!"[3]

In-flight refueling was a routine evolution in naval

aviation by 1964, easier in daytime than at night, of course. Such specialized skills as aerial refueling, carrier landings, overwater navigation, and precise weapons delivery marked naval aviators as perhaps the most accomplished of fliers. (Though our air force cousins never evidenced any reluctance in arguing that point!)

The entire package—of ships, aircraft, and fliers—was aimed at serving the objectives of U.S. national interest, however defined. Specifically, the strike carrier force had two primary goals: control of the sea and projection of power ashore. Secondary missions included what navies have done since there were navies: show the flag and maintain "presence." The latter had much to do with deterrence. If you show a strong enough presence, you may not have to project power; often the implied threat is sufficient.

The critical background of naval aviation was formed in World War II and Korea. In 1964, only eleven years had passed since the Korean Conflict. Many active aviators and most officers at squadron commander level and above had had fleet experience during that fracas, if not actual combat experience.

Naval aviation's institutional experience from Korea had many similarities with the war brewing in the Tonkin Gulf. Both were sparked by communist aggression. Both were early cast as no-win contests owing to political decisions by the national leadership. Concern for Soviet and Communist Chinese reaction was an overriding factor in both Korea and Vietnam, with some justification in the former, but apparently with almost none in the latter. Chinese/Soviet concern was uppermost in the minds of Johnson administration officials. Nixon's actions—mining and bombing previously off-limit targets—did *not* result in China/USSR escalating the war.

Neither war was a naval war, so the carrier's sole

purpose in each was power projection ashore. This
involved both direct air support to ground forces and
strikes against enemy logistical and occasionally industrial
targets. But as we shall see, the rules of engagement (ROE) attained specific levels in Korea and extremely specific levels in Vietnam, thus imposing restraints
on the proper application of airpower. Not only were
targets affected but tactics as well: ordnance, strike
timing, even run-in headings were among the elements
strictly controlled. The result reduced the military chain
of command to little more than a communications channel.

Overseeing the tactical control of Asian operations
was Task Force 77, at first in the Sea of Japan and
Yellow Sea flanking the Korean peninsula and later in
the Tonkin Gulf off Indochina. Carriers rotated in and
out of TF 77 as available or as need arose, with carrier
division (CarDiv) commanders alternating as the task
force commander (CTF 77). Seldom were four carriers
on hand at any one time. (The command structure and
division of labor will be examined later.)

Air wing operations were also similar in Korea and
Vietnam. Deckload strikes upwards of thirty aircraft)
were flown against briefed targets in addition to cyclic
operations employing smaller formations. "Cyclic ops"
constituted the majority of carrier sorties, as there was
more requirement for these flexible missions. In Vietnam,
specific targets such as railyards or major bridges were
objects of Alpha strikes, while Rolling Thunder operations cycled smaller free-lancing missions in search of
specified types of targets. The shorter endurance time
of unrefueled jets mandated more intense schedules in
Korea and Vietnam than carrier aviators had known in
World War II. A typical cycle time in 1944 was four
hours from launch to recovery. Twenty years later,
cyclic ops were run, as a rule, on a ninety-minute basis.

Air operations were conducted almost entirely without threat to the carriers off Korea and Vietnam, although anti-submarine operations were maintained as a precaution in Korea. We owned the sea and mainly we owned the air. We owned the air particularly in Korea, where only five carrier-based aircraft were lost to hostile planes.[4] In such a situation, it should have been possible to achieve almost anything within the technical limits of aircraft and ordnance, but such was not the case.

There are two major reasons airpower did not achieve its potential in these Asian wars. First, the relative crudeness of communist logistic and communications systems allowed any damaged segments to be repaired virtually overnight. Second, the political limits placed on targeting and tactics prevented dealing with the source of supply. If we had choked off supplies and munitions at their entry into the theater, we would not have had to chase down individual trucks (or oxcarts or bicycles) on their way through the combat zone.

Ironically, the correct procedure eventually was applied in North Vietnam. But by 1972, when Haiphong and other ports were closed by mining, it was far too late. Public support for the war had eroded to a point where disengagement became the preferred alternative to victory or stalemate. Thus, airpower's potential for success against North Vietnam was lost to view. The "failure" of airpower remains one of the enduring myths of the Vietnam War, and one that we shall examine in this book.

The pilot's immediate concern centered on the risk imposed by the enemy. Although few U.S. planes were actually shot down by MiGs, the danger was always there. Far and away the greatest cause of loss to navy aircraft in both Korea and Vietnam was the airplane's oldest enemy: gunfire.

Over Korea, the threat was similar to that in World

Grumman F9F-8 Cougar

War II: barrage fire from both small arms and major-caliber antiaircraft artillery (AAA), occasionally radar-directed. Over North Vietnam, the new surface-to-air missiles (SAMs) forced attacking aircraft to fly low, thereby exposing the planes to fire from otherwise obsolete guns.

Korea was the first conflict in which jet aircraft operated from carriers, as witnessed by the Grumman F9F series and the McDonnell F2H. In Vietnam, carrier aircraft already in the inventory (much as the F9F and F2H from Korea) were inaugurated to combat while other types such as the A-6 and A-7 joined the fleet in time of war. More sophisticated ordnance, such as standoff weapons and antiradiation missiles, also appeared. For weapons as for warriors, the only meaningful test is trial by combat, and Korea and Vietnam provided that test.

Despite the similarities, Korea and Vietnam differed greatly at the strategic and tactical levels. The conflict in Korea began abruptly, on 25 June 1950, when the

U.S. Navy had only six fleet carriers in commission and just one in the theater. Vietnam, in contrast, was a long process of gradual escalation, and there was no shortage of ships or aircraft.

Unlike North Korea, North Vietnam experienced no invasions by naval aviation's long-time partner, the amphibious force. For North Vietnam there was no Inchon or Wonsan.

Threat levels were considerably higher in North Vietnam than in Korea. SAMs appeared in the 1960s, and aerial combat "Up North" was a genuine concern from 1965 to 1973.* The Vietnam War, which lasted almost three times as long as the Korean Conflict, had three times the number of losses in air combat but five times the number of victories over enemy aircraft. Hence there was more aerial activity in Vietnam and greater opportunity for loss.[5]

Another major difference between the two conflicts was in the role of electronic warfare. ECM aircraft such as EA-1 Skyraiders (AS-4Ns in Korea) flew in both wars, with largely the same vacuum-tube technology, but dedicated jet ECM platforms such as the EA-3 and eventually the supersophisticated EA-6B participated in Vietnam.

Since Korea tremendous strides had been made in the capabilities of radar and communications. Surface-to-air missiles relied almost entirely upon radar tracking and guidance before electro-optical systems became available, and a large proportion of North Vietnam's AAA batteries also were radar-directed. Consequently, electronic countermeasures assumed more importance than before.

---

*"Up North" was a common phrase of the period, used to denote North Vietnam. It reflects a sentiment as much as a geographical area, appearing, for example, in a U.S. Air Force toast, "To our comrades Up North," meaning "To the POWs in North Vietnamese prisons."

Another tactical difference was in the composition of carrier air wings. In Korea a fleet carrier usually had aboard two jet fighter squadrons and three propeller fighter-bomber squadrons. At no time did Panthers and Banshees represent more than half of a carrier air group during Korea. But at the beginning of the Vietnam War, the situation was almost the reverse. A-1s still flew from most carriers, but they were already being phased out in favor of A-4s. The higher threat levels Up North, where conventional wisdom had it that "speed is life," forced the retirement of Skyraiders. From mid-1968 on, all carrier-based fighter, attack, and reconnaissance aircraft were jet-powered. However, propeller-driven aircraft still performed the early-warning and antisubmarine functions without hardship. E-1s, E-2s, and S-2s were all propeller-driven.

The land war in Vietnam involved more coordination with our allies than did the war as fought from the sea. In Korea, British and Australian carriers had shared the duty with American flattops. In fact, during the early phase, they constituted half the carrier force offshore. But by 1964 the British Commonwealth could not have spared carriers for service in the Tonkin Gulf even if it had so desired. American carrier forces, however, were able to meet the need, even if some ships were hard-pressed with continuous deployments.

Task Force 77 ships were a good deal less mobile off Indochina than they had been in Korean waters. This was largely due to geography, as Korea is a peninsula and Indochina borders almost wholly on the Tonkin Gulf. The U.S. carriers therefore operated in just two spots—"Yankee Station" south of Hainan for strikes against North Vietnam and "Dixie Station" off South Vietnam. From Dixie Station, strikes were also launched into Laos and Cambodia.

By the end of the Korean War, jets were becoming

more numerous and more capable, and supercarriers were about to appear. In a sense—because of the axial-deck carrier and propeller-driven Skyraiders and Corsairs—Korea was World War II again, only with jets.

With modified *Essex*-class carriers becoming more available and the *Forrestals* entering service, naval aviation entered a decade of relative stasis interrupted by spurts of remarkable progress. By 1960 the ships and aircraft—and many of the aviators—that would be used against North Vietnam were in the fleet, building experience.

But the peace of the 1950s was deceptive. From 1954 through 1959, Soviet or Chinese aircraft attacked U.S. Navy patrol planes at least once a year, and they shot down several. Air Force and civilian planes also were victims of harassment and attack.

Communistic regimes also were being established close to the United States. The Cuban revolution of 1959 presaged changes in Latin America that continue to this day. Whether stronger measures earlier would have averted the problems will never be known. But the 1960-64 period brought about a considerable rethinking in naval aviation.

Carrier aviation enjoyed success in the Mediterranean (an American lake in those days) through support of the Marine landings in Lebanon in 1958. Four years later, with President Kennedy's blockade during the Cuban missile crisis, naval aviation again felt success when eight carriers enforced the barrier against delivery of Soviet nuclear missiles to Cuba.

In the long run, the United States probably lost more than it gained in that confrontation. Aside from unpublicized concessions to the Soviets in return for their removal of the ICBMs from Cuba, the Russians were provided a humiliating but harmless lesson in seapower. They learned the lesson and began constructing a modern deep-water navy that has now grown to global proportions.

When the Bay of Pigs fiasco occurred eighteen months before the blockade, carrier airmen were also on hand. As if in anticipation of procedures over North Vietnam, Skyhawk pilots of Attack Squadron 34 watched the amphibious operation founder for lack of air cover. The puny Cuban air force, unopposed within visual distance of the orbiting Blue Blasters flying off *Essex*, met no more opposition than a steely-eyed stare. Even that was enough to dissuade one Cuban pilot from finishing off a crippled B-26, and the episode became a legend in VA-34.[6]

Actually, Atlantic Fleet pilots were well acquainted with Cuban waters owing to the curious situation that left the naval base and air station at Guantanamo Bay in American hands. "Gitmo" was frequently the site of live-fire exercises before Castro came to power, and some missions were conducted thereafter. One of the amusing diversions in those days was to make a low-level supersonic pass along the fence that divided the base from the rest of the island. Such antics frequently elicited a nastygram from Fidel, which was well received by all hands.

Despite the apparent peace of the Caribbean, those of us flying in AirLant knew that the Soviets and East Germans were bringing Cuban pilots up to speed in MiG-17s and, later, in MiG-21s. Inevitably, we began to tangle. One episode from the Christmas holidays of 1964 will illustrate.*

---

*The stories recounted in this book reflect for the most part the experiences or knowledge of Commander John Nichols, USN (Ret.). When "I" is used, it refers to Cdr. Nichols.

Cuban MiGs occasionally harassed U.S. patrol planes beyond the twelve-mile limit, following a pattern established by the Soviets and Chinese. Fighter Squadron 62, between deployments at NAS Key West, Florida, was maintaining a duty section of new F-8Es in rotation with other squadrons. My section leader and I were on call when the horn sounded.

Two MiG-17s had made themselves obnoxious to a navy surveillance aircraft in international airspace south of Havana. The jets pulled up in front of the patrol plane, close aboard, rocking it with their turbulence. Our section scrambled and was gear-up in ninety seconds, booming south in afterburner.

When we arrived, the MiGs had turned for home, leaving an angry and shaken navy crew behind. The Crusader leader, one of the best carrier aviators I ever knew, dropped behind the lead MiG at a mile-and-a-half while I tracked the wingman. The Cubans were blissfully unaware of us; they made no turns or evasive maneuvers.

I heard the AIM-9D's tracking signal in my earphones. It was a good tone; the missile was working perfectly. The leader called our controller: "What do you want me to do?" A pause, then, "Stand by." I was incredulous. A perfect setup was being lost to indecision. When we reached SAM range offshore, the controller radioed, "Suggest you come port." We broke off and returned to base.

I was disappointed, more so when we were later ushered into the office of the rear admiral commanding the district. We found him on the phone to Washington. When he hung up, he told us we had passed up a beautiful opportunity. The MiGs were blatantly in the wrong, well outside Cuban waters, and we could have fired. But the F-8 leader, who was really too nice a

MiG-17

fellow to be a fighter pilot, had missed a chance to
teach the bad guys a lesson.

Years later, my section leaders still thought we had
acted properly. He didn't want two dead men on his
conscience. It was three and a half years before I saw a
MiG-17 again, and then it was flown by a twenty-three-
year-old Vietnamese (his age noted on a biographical
sheet provided by an intelligence officer) who tried to
kill the photo pilot I was escorting.

This episode was not the only U.S. encounter with
MiGs. Once in a while some of our pilots got a look at
MiG-21s when they flew at contrail altitudes. On these
rare occasions the Crusaders maintained a three-mile
lateral separation as each side looked over the opposition.

The 21 was a sleek, attractive Mach-two fighter that appeared in 1956. For years it was overrated by our intelligence people, but the F-8 community practiced hard to counter the main threat aircraft. When practice ended and it was war Up North, we were ready.

However, naval aviation was not entirely ready for the air-defense environment that quickly evolved in North Vietnam. This was largely because we misread the lessons of Korea and Cuba. The main reason was the surface-to-air missile. At least two American aircraft had been lost to Soviet SA-2s before Vietnam. Undoubtedly there were others, but we knew of only two: Gary Powers's U-2 over Russia and another U-2 over Cuba during the missile crisis. Because of these incidents, the analysts insisted the SAM was the primary threat. After all, if it could knock down high-flying airplanes like the U-2, what chance did we have in tactical aircraft at 20,000 to 30,000 feet? So the conventional wisdom held that air strikes would be made below the minimum effective range of Soviet missiles. This altitude was variously reported up to 3,500 feet, and we came in for a nasty surprise on that point a few years later.

In order to put bombs on target at low level, it is necessary to slow down the ordnance so the bomber isn't hit by the blast. Most types of conventional bombs will throw fragments two thousand feet into the air, threatening the aircraft. Ordnance engineers designed the retarded bomb, with fins that deploy at the tail upon release and slow the weapon's descent, allowing the aircraft time to get away from the blast. Mark 82 Snakeyes were the most common bomb of this category.

The problem was that each trailing aircraft was exposed to bomb fragments if bombs were dropped at the usual intervals. So the low, flat approach required greater spacing between aircraft, meaning that the strike group spent more time over the target. Consequently, the opposition had more time to react and better prospects of shooting down a couple of airplanes.

Although these tactics usually put us below effective SAM range, they exposed us to all manner of AAA and smallarms. But the analysts had an answer for that, too. They believed that fast jets could not be tracked; an aircraft making 450 to 500 knots, they argued, posed an almost impossible target for any gunner to acquire and follow in the time available.

But it wasn't necessary to track an airplane. The old-fashioned barrage system of pattern gunfire worked just fine. We should have remembered that from Korea, but the U.S. Navy lacked an institutional memory. We rediscovered the hard truth about barrage antiaircraft fire over North Vietnam. The situation was compounded by what many aviators feared—the longer time over target offered the defenders more chances to shoot, and the early air strikes Up North suffered the highest loss rates of the entire war.

These procedures were ingrained in the tactical aviation community, not only by doctrine but by operational experience. During 1963–64, at least four contingency strikes were armed and launched against prebriefed targets in Cuba. I flew at least four such missions. The reason for these strikes was not made clear to the aircrews. We merely had to assume there was sufficient intelligence to warrant the operations, which were flown under cover of scheduled weapons practice at the Pine Castle bombing range. In fact, there was nothing "scheduled" about them. The usual procedure was to call the aviators at home or in quarters at about 2000 with instructions to arrive for briefing at 0200. Upon arrival at Cecil Field, the aviators saw all the activity: airplanes were being towed or taxied to fueling and arming areas, ordnance was being loaded. It looked like preparation for a combat mission. In addition, the aviators were almost entirely instructors from their respective communities along the Atlantic coast—A-1s, A-4s, A-3 tankers, F-4s, and F-8s. In short, the first team.

Navy squadrons were assigned the eastern half of Cuba, mainly targeted against airfields and suspected missile sites. Air Force units were also involved, but to what extent we neither knew nor cared. We were far too busy with own planning and preparations.

Guantanamo Bay was the alternate landing field in case of any battle damage that precluded return to Florida. The two runways were 4,000 and 8,000 feet long, but preparations were in hand for using much less room. Arresting gear was installed on the runways in case Cuban artillery or bombs rendered portions of the runways unusable. The F-8 pilots reckoned they could land in 2,000 feet and take off in 3,000 feet if necessary. But operating under those conditions, right under the guns of the Cubans, would have been tough. The prospect evoked in my mind images of what Henderson Field ·at Guadalcanal must have been like.*

We launched the equivalent of a deckload strike— about thirty airplanes, with most of the fighters doubling as bombers. In deference to the SAMs, we would have gone in at about 500 feet with our Snakeyes amidst whatever AAA and smallarms the Cubans could put up. It probably would have been substantial.

---

*For a full account of the aircraft and the fliers who saved this embattled island, read *The Cactus Air Force* by Thomas G. Miller, Jr. Another volume in the Bantam War Book Series.

Four times we manned up and four times we headed south, expecting to hit our assigned targets. But four times, after passing Andros Island, we turned as instructed and dumped our ordnance at Pine Castle instead. There was little follow-up information, so we never really knew what prompted the strikes to be launched or aborted.

These tactics were in effect when the shooting started in the Tonkin Gulf. Perhaps if we'd actually completed one of those Cuban missions we'd have learned our lesson relatively inexpensively. As it was, the tuition was deferred.

The Cuban experience, both actual and tentative, had considerable influence on the tactics in vogue at the beginning of the Vietnam War. It's an influence that has not received much acknowledgment in the literature. Yet the limited operations around the island, the advent of SAMs and their early success, and the occasional MiG encounters all combined to solidify existing concepts and doctrines.

At some point, someone should have asked, "Wait a minute. We know what the theory is for this particular set of circumstances. But what if the real world or the world of the near future doesn't reflect these circumstances? What then?" The sad fact is that nobody asked that question. Instead, we proceeded on the convenient assumption that the next war would resemble Korea and events shortly following.

Any system needs internal checks, an institutional devil's advocate to pose questions contrary to the conventional wisdom. In that respect, the lack of foresight was a failing at a far higher level than in the air wings or at the carrier divisions.

In defense of the aviators and strike planners in the "Tonkin Gulf Yacht Club," the learning curve was high.

It usually is in a war. After the initial nasty surprises in Operations Flaming Dart and Pierce Arrow, measures were taken to reevaluate existing doctrines, to adjust to that real world which nobody had perceived one or two years previously.

2

RULES OF ENGAGEMENT

There is only one rule in war: one must win.

—*General Vo Nguyen Giap*

Comedian Bill Cosby had a routine in the late 1960s that speculated on the presentation of Revolutionary War tactics. Cosby cast the opposing generals as team captains receiving pregame instructions from the referee. The routine went something like this:

> Cap'n Washington, meet Cap'n Cornwallis. Cap'n Cornwallis, meet Cap'n Washington. Cap'n Cornwallis, your team gets to wear bright red coats, stand in nice straight lines, and march around in the open. Cap'n Washington, your team gets to hide behind trees, shoot from behind rocks, and run away if the redcoats get too close. Good luck to both of you.

Whether intentional or not, it provides a lucid analogy to the rules of engagement in Vietnam.

The bombing campaign against North Vietnam was called Rolling Thunder. The name originated with an old gospel hymn, the title of which must have met the approval of the most irreligious of all egotistical tactical aviators: *How Great Thou Art*.

From the inception of Rolling Thunder in 1965 until mid-1972 the published ROE for tac air Up North changed relatively little. However, individual air wings often made their own amendments. So Rolling Thunder evolved into a complex situation, lasting as it did for eight years with different emphasis in different areas at different times. Today, ROE documentation is hard to come by—surprising in light of all the paperwork the operation engendered.

The central theme in this ill-defined effort was to keep civilian casualties to a minimum. Lyndon Johnson boasted that "they can't bomb an outhouse without my approval," and thought that was something to be proud of.[1] But whether one regards that situation as laudable or ludicrous, the fact is it didn't work and it didn't make sense. At times it seemed as if we were trying to see how much ordnance we could drop on North Vietnam without disturbing the country's way of life.

The overriding contradiction was between the stated purpose of forcing Hanoi to the bargaining table as the bomb line moved slowly north, while placing self-restraint upon the level of violence. The contradiction was unresolved or ignored for seven years and was finally settled only in the last eight months of American involvement.

Targeting was essentially limited to communications networks—roads, canals, and bridges—and petroleum-oil-lubricant (POL) storage facilities. Restricted areas included most cities and a thirty-mile buffer zone along the Chinese border. In addition, North Vietnamese defenses were often off-limits to attack, which complicated air strike planning and execution. A few examples will illustrate the point: that the ROE meant we couldn't properly suppress the threat.

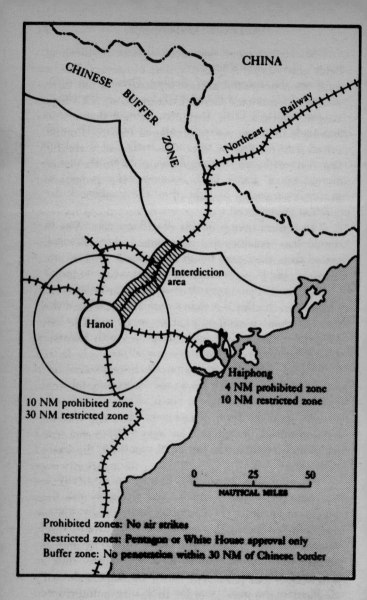

Hanoi-Haiphong Targeting Restrictions 1965–68

No strikes were permitted against northern airfields until April 1967, for a variety of reasons. The one most often presented at air-wing level was the thrice-weekly International Control Commission (ICC) flight. Largely overlooked in accounts of a war that set new standards of irony, the International Control Commission, established to "enforce" the 1954 treaty, dutifully followed its charter, flying in and out of North Vietnam on published schedules to monitor the progress of French-Vietnamese accords.

For diplomatic reasons, it wouldn't do to have an ICC DC-3 smeared on the ramp at Gia Lam. Why this should have prevented us from taking out other fields remained unexplained. Scuttlebutt had it that other factors worked against airfield strikes. They included a reluctance to place Soviets or other "neutrals" at risk, and there was a bizarre theory that if we bombed their bases the MiGs would pull north into China. The latter would actually have benefitted us on two points: it would have placed NVAF interceptors much farther from our operating areas, and would have allowed us to establish CAPs easily positioned to intercept them southbound.

It's possible in retrospect to see how the Washington managers and analysts may have been unconcerned about losing some planes to MiGs. After all, the United States was never in danger of losing air superiority over the North. But what if some enterprising MiG driver had used the immunity we granted him to launch from a coastal airfield and seriously damage or even sink one of our ships? In such an instance there would surely have arisen an unholy stink about the ROE and our hands-off airfields policy. Perhaps that is why such an attack never took place. The North Vietnamese shrewdly declined that option in order to ensure uninterrupted use of their northernmost fighter bases.

SAM sites were another case in point. Secretary of Defense Robert Strange McNamara knew that Soviet technicians were installing and often operating the new surface-to-air missile batteries. Because of concern about harming "neutral" Soviets, U.S. tac air crews were ordered by the Pentagon to pass up these sites even when they were vulnerable during construction. One F-4 squadron commander off USS *Midway* actually watched the SAM site being built that eventually shot him down in 1965.[2]

Eventually there were more than one hundred SAM sites in and around Hanoi, and about 30 to 40 percent remained off-limits throughout the war because of their proximity to "civilian" facilities. The most notorious example was the capital's big soccer stadium, which safely housed a multitude of launchers. Finally, in 1968, most sites that fired and were detected could be engaged as long as hitting them posed no hazard to civilians.

Once in a while things went awry. Since the opposition quickly learned where it could and could not place antiaircraft batteries subject to attack, many were sited in populated areas. But the thirty-five-foot SA-2s sometimes went berserk upon launch, thrashing around town at street level like a rocket-propelled bulldozer. Not surprisingly, the old neighborhood underwent urban renewal on such occasions, much to the aviators' amusement. But the Vietnamese, never ones to pass up a propaganda coup, usually recovered their poise with a convincingly outraged display of the Yankee air pirates' handiwork in bombing civilian areas.

Antiaircraft artillery sites were often accorded immunity as well. But gun crews possessed an additional advantage when afloat. Chinese communist ships frequently mounted 20- or 37mm guns on their sterns, and Haiphong harbor was often full of merchantmen from the People's Republic of China. U.S. aircraft passing over Haiphong were nearly always taken under fire by the Chinese, in total confidence that retaliation would never ensue.[3] A few Russian ships also joined in at odd intervals.

Any shipping was immune to attack except under special circumstances. Even ships anchored offshore were restricted targets, though they might be visibly off-loading munitions. Barges ferrying stores toward shore were permitted targets if six hundred meters from the ship, but this policy was not as generous as it may seem. The communists inevitably conducted such operations at night, and it was impossible to identify the barges from among the thousands of smallcraft plying the coastal waterways.

We could attack a boat only when that vessel overtly interfered with a rescue attempt. If a downed flier was in danger of being captured or run down, the offending craft could be engaged and destroyed. Few such instances were recorded. A tacit understanding grew up between the Vietnamese sailors and American pilots: largely live and let live.

Few people realize how crowded the Tonkin Gulf actually was. Our task force usually operated about 150 miles offshore, but the gulf was plied by thousands of smallcraft, mostly fishing boats and junks. Some were powered but most were under sail. In accordance with the law of the sea, these little vessels had the right of way over a man-of-war. But beyond that, U.S. Navy captains were never permitted to interfere with the ability of the North Vietnamese to feed themselves. There was to be no cutting of fishing nets, no swamping smallcraft by passing too close.

Most of these vessels were family-owned and harmless. But a good many were armed. First-tour aviators always came back in a surly mood from their initial night missions: "You should have seen all the muzzle flashes from smallarms when we headed west!" The old hands merely shrugged their shoulders. "Don't sweat it. Those boats shoot at us in daytime, too, but the flashes don't show up."

The greater danger came not from whatever antiquated guns the fishermen took to sea; it was in the form of early warning. A U.S. carrier group can't go anywhere on any ocean without drawing the inevitable Soviet "trawler" as a tagalong. Junks and fishing boats also carried radios, but the Russians possessed far better communications and radar equipment. Every time Task Force 77 launched aircraft, air defense in downtown Hanoi got word within minutes.

The Soviets sometimes took more active measures. Like the smallcraft, they could position themselves for right of way over warships. Frequently the Russian vessels deliberately crossed the bow of a carrier engaged in flight operations, forcing the CV to alter course. This resulted in a delay in launch or a wave-off for the plane in the groove, depending upon the situation. Eventually we hammered out an arrangement with the Soviets on such matters, for the situation existed worldwide. It would have been only a matter of time until a collision occurred.

It was possible to gain a little revenge on some occasions. Phantom, Crusader, or Vigilante pilots fortunate enough to launch while a Russian ship lay directly upwind could make the most of the situation. They simply remained in after-burner at mast height and flew directly over the vessel, accelerating to Mach one. The sound, feel, and sheer concussion of a supersonic aircraft streaking fifty feet overhead must be experienced to comprehend. It felt good to rattle their cage.

While we were distracted in the gulf, the most worthwhile target in North Vietnam lay untouched. The

Haiphong docks, eminently lucrative as a choke point, were never hit. They covered a huge area, with as many as eight or nine railway tracks supporting mobile cranes. Again, political considerations prevented us from destroying these easily neutralized facilities. The presence of Soviet-, Chinese- and frequently European-registered ships was considered too sensitive a matter for military action. This despite the fact that more of North Vietnam's supplies entered the country at that point than anywhere else.

Another lesser restriction was Do San Lighthouse, jutting eastward on a small spit offshore. Though it was probably not operational, it remained off-limits because of its passive duty as an aid to navigation. But frustrated carrier pilots frequently expended remaining ammunition or rockets on Do San anyway—"just because they told us not to," explained one aviator. Year by year, the old lighthouse became more chipped and chinked, some saying it visibly leaned one way or the other from the hammering of 20mm and Zunis.

The communist Chinese island of Hainan also figured in the ROE. This thirteen-thousand-square-mile island dominates the Tonkin Gulf geographically and militarily. It boasted a number of airfields, and PRC MiG-17s or 19s frequently harassed and sometimes attacked navy aircraft. Despite such provocations, no retaliatory measures were authorized from Washington. We were obliged to honor the twelve-mile limit to the extent that not even search-and-rescue flights were permitted within that boundary. At least one naval aviator was abandoned to his fate in Hainan waters "on orders from beyond the Pentagon."[4]

However, overflights of Hainan were not entirely unknown. Usually these happened through a combination of poor weather and radio failure. I always will remember an episode in 1967, when flying off the *Ti-*

conderoga in Air Wing 19. A *Tico* Skyraider, flown by a blissfully ignorant "nugget"—a new aviator—wandered northward on top of the cloud deck, smack over Hainan. The A-1 had lost radio contact with the ship so my outbound F-8 was vectored to an intercept to bring the errant youngster home. Slowed up and dirtied up, I pulled alongside and tried to impress him with the seriousness of the situation. Low and slow, beautifully silhouetted against the clouds, was no place to be if MiGs appeared.

Incredibly, the A-1 playfully turned to me, initiating an offensive scissors. He wanted to play dogfighter deep in communist airspace, without communication with his ship or other aircraft!

In truth, the befuddled Spad driver had no idea where he was. Once he consented to be led home, his skipper launched into a world-class tail-chewing that ended with the nugget being grounded approximately forever. But it's only funny in retrospect.

F-8 Crusader

Operations over North Vietnam were administered by dividing the country into six areas called route packages. From south to north they were Route Packs I through IV. Route Pack V covered the western portion of the wide northern area, while VI included Hanoi and points east to the coast. Route Pack VI, the real hotspot, was divided into VIA in the west and VIB to the east, along the Northeast Railway out of Hanoi. The navy was assigned Route Packs II, III, IV, and VIB, the last featuring Haiphong.

Missions into any route pack were closely monitored by command levels in-theater or in Washington. Until 1966, for instance, no strikes were run into Route Pack II without forward air controllers, or FACs. At that time the North Vietnamese defenses were rather thin, but the FAC procedure indicated a poor understanding of air ops north of the demilitarized zone (DMZ). The FACs did excellent work in South Vietnam, where their low-and-slow methods were made possible by low levels of risk. But the air-defense environment north of the 17th Parallel was different.

Air Force strikes in Route Pack V were limited, but not to the extent of the nit-picking control in VI. This was partially because few good targets existed in V; the major transport and logistical centers were in VI, extended down the coast through IV. Nearly all the navy's maximum-effort (Alpha) strikes were flown in Route Pack VIB, usually under Pentagon control or higher.

Alpha strikes, though, were the exception. Rolling Thunders were the ordinary day-in, day-out missions, and they were administered at CarDiv or CTF levels. It was largely a matter of matching approved target systems with available information from photoreconnaissance or other intelligence sources.

Tactical aviators from World War II would recognize Rolling Thunders as armed reconnaissance missions—

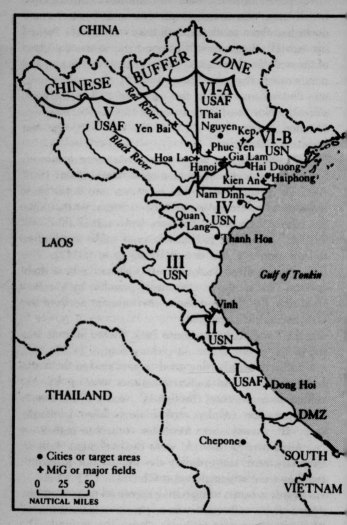

North Vietnam: Route Packages and Notable Features

"road recces" and the like. But there was a difference over North Vietnam. Instead of merely flying up and down highways or canals, trolling for whatever turned up, carrier pilots Up North were seeking specific types of targets. One week it might be trucks or barges, the next week perhaps bridges.

Not only were operating areas subject to Washington's approval but so too were details such as ordnance. For much of the war, as an example, no 2,000-pound bombs could be used without specific permission from CTF-77. Actually, few one-ton bombs were available, and there were periods of bomb shortages. At one point we had to buy back from Germany large stocks of ordnance previously sold under NATO agreements. When it came to heavy ordnance, Commander in Chief Pacific (CinCPac) might approve such details, but more often the decision was retained at Pentagon level.

New or exotic weapons were also subject to tight control. Walleye, the TV-guided glide-bomb, was a good example. First employed in 1967, the Walleye was accurate and efficient, lacking only sufficient power to take out really tough targets such as the Thanh Hoa Bridge.

Other aviation ordnance was permitted in the South but banned Up North. Napalm was a case in point. We refrained from using "hell-jelly" in North Vietnam, which was too bad. Napalm, while inefficient in high-angle dives, could have been a useful weapon in some cases—Rescue Combat Air Patrols (ResCAPs) or in attacks on isolated gun positions or buildings that permitted a low, shallow-angle approach.

Cluster bomb units (CBUs) were another example. These were bomblets within a large cannister, designed to deploy at preset altitudes above the ground. The higher the altitude, the wider the dispersion but the thinner the coverage. Some ordnance enthusiasts claimed

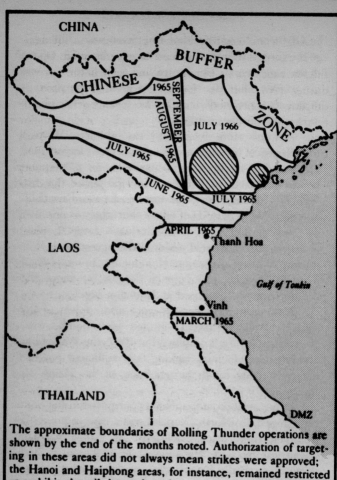

The approximate boundaries of Rolling Thunder operations are shown by the end of the months noted. Authorization of targeting in these areas did not always mean strikes were approved; the Hanoi and Haiphong areas, for instance, remained restricted or prohibited until the war's end.

The Bombs Line's Migration North

the CBUs could not only take out guncrews, but damage the guns as well. It remained largely unproved. One of the few times CBUs were employed early in the war was during 1967, but not for their intended purpose. A diligent, bespectacled young sailor working at his photo-interpreter job about 0300 one morning made a major find. In the southern part of Route Pack III, well camouflaged in a wooded area, was the biggest POL stash yet discovered. A thin-skinned target of that sort was made to order for CBUs, which possessed the dual advantages of moderate penetration plus incendiary characteristics. The strikes went off without a hitch—not even any battle damage to the planes—and the POL plant spewed smoke to more than 10,000 feet for six days.

But the potential effectiveness of antipersonnel weapons such as napalm and CBUs was badly denigrated for most of the war Up North. Political sensitivity towards inflicting casualties diminished or deprived our defense-suppression efforts.

The State Department was particularly touchy about hurting enemy or "neutral" people. For quite a while, in 1967 and 1968, State was actually approving or specifying the bomb loads against certain targets. Presumably it was acceptable to kill a few North Vietnamese, so long as we didn't use too much ordnance in the process, but no harm was to befall any Soviet, People's Republic of China (PRC), or other visiting personnel.

Some Americans flatly refused to believe the State Department was involved in such decision making. About this time—1967 or 1968—a political science lecturer at the University of Oregon harangued against aviators who bombed North Vietnam. When confronted with the fact that diplomats were determining much of the ordnance loads, the professor retorted, "Oh, my brother is an air force pilot and he says the same thing. But I don't believe him, either."[5]

Another example of political meddling in tactical matters concerned bridge approaches. For seven years, perhaps 80 percent of all permitted targets in the North were bridges, as communications routes were prominent on the approved "hit lists.' But if you're bombing a bridge, you either hit it or you make it wet. Near-misses seldom harm a bridge as it is immune to concussion, unlike a ship or building.

Therefore, the correct run-in heading (assuming adequate topography) is just a few degrees off the bridge's axis. The intent is to walk a stick of bombs at a slight diagonal across the target, allowing straddles on either side and—presumably—one or two hits. A perfectly aligned dive angle with the length of the target affords no margin for error at all—a string of bombs will nearly always fall to one side or the other.

The people approving tactical procedures, however, balked at the correct method. They'd been told that in dive bombing, range errors generally exceed deflection, which is true. Therefore, with an attack angle parallel to the bridge, chances existed for "overs" to strike the far shore rather than the river or ravine. And where there were bridges, there were roads leading onto and off those bridges. And, by extension, where there were roads there might be people; civilian people.

So, DOD and the White House variously directed that run-in headings be perpendicular to the target. That is, in the direction of the river instead of the direction of the bridge. This procedure accomplished several things.

First, it flew in the face of the entire experience of bombing bridges. British pilots in the First World War quickly discovered the correct method, and even today there are a few octogenarians around who recall angling their SE-5s into dives a few degrees off target heading. God bless them; we could have used a few in Route Pack IV.

Perpendicular Approach

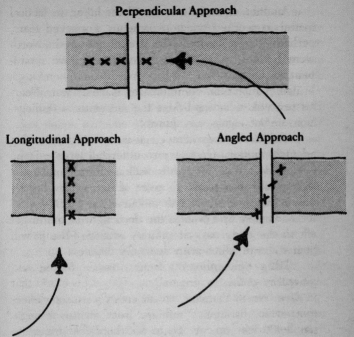

Longitudinal Approach

Angled Approach

Representative Results of Attack Headings on Bridges

Second, a perpendicular approach made the target nearly impossible to hit. Instead of shooting for a very long target, you are suddenly confronted with an exceedingly thin one. And remember, near-misses don't count. Bridge busting bears no relationship to horseshoes.

Last, but certainly not least, you are now beautifully positioned as a target. Tac air objectives come in all sizes, shapes, and descriptions, but they have one thing in common: if they're worth bombing, they're worth defending. In cases where the opposition knew from experience that run-in headings would likely be perpendicular to the span, AAA defenses could be placed for optimum accuracy. If batteries were located upstream and down, on both banks, the bomber would be exposed in profile from both sides as it entered that predictable, straight dive. The aircraft and crew losses incurred on missions flown under these ROE were often unnecessary.

Another primary communications link was trucks. This fact was recognized from the inception of Rolling Thunder, but, again, any possibly effective action was hampered by the overriding concern for civilian casualties. Only *military* trucks were authorized targets, and they could only be hit a safe distance from populated areas or very near roads. In point of fact, nearly *every* truck in North Vietnam was military. But the tweedy decision makers who evolved this doctrine were a throwback to the early days of military aviation—the Billy Mitchell era in which army and navy disasters (such as the airship *Shenandoah**) were directly linked to nonaviators' orders to airmen.

Over North Vietnam, tac air crews were somehow expected to distinguish military from civilian trucks from 3,000 feet up, at 500 to 550 knots. A difficult-enough proposition, even ignoring the fact that no clear distinction between types of trucks existed. The entire nation was mobilized for war, and everything that moved—from bicycles to buffalo—contributed to the North Vietnamese war effort. Furthermore, aviators noted enemy trucks parked in "civilian" villages that were immune to attack under the ROE.

Bicycles were an interesting logistical tool in the communist inventory. Not until 1968 or later was the Hanoi bicycle plant hit. Aircrews returning to the States

---

*In September 1925, USN airship *Shenandoah* (ZR-1) was ordered to fly in poor weather, despite the CO's objection. Severe winds tore the ship apart, killing the CO and thirteen others. Nine months later Congress enacted legislation requiring aviation units be commanded by rated airmen, avoiding repetition of the *Shenandoah* tragedy.

were met with reactions from mirth to horror if they dared mention this target. But bikes kept a large portion of the tonnage moving down the Ho Chi Minh Trail. They weren't ridden, but pushed. A standard bicycle could carry about one hundred fifty pounds of food, supplies, and ammunition. In 1942 Japanese troops had ridden tireless bikes on their rims to rapidly encircle Singapore.

The on-again-off-again bombing campaign was marked by periodic halts for official and unofficial talks or for "goodwill" gestures during Tet and the Christian holidays. But they seemed aimed more at the American antiwar movement than at Hanoi.[6] During stand-downs, the task force withdrew deeper into the gulf to await developments. Ordinary sorties were maintained, however. RF-8s and RA-5s conducted weather and tac recon flights, which could be authorized at CTF-77 level. The same applied to Barrier Combat Air Patrols (BarCAPs) off Haiphong. Otherwise, Pentagon, State Department, or White House authorization was required for offensive operation.

Photo recce missions were the most feared among aviators during such periods. A single fighter accompanied the recon plane without nearly MiGCAP, standby SAR helos, or any other support. It wasn't certain whether helicopters could have been cleared inland during stand-downs, anyway, as they could have been interpreted in some quarters as "offensive" in nature.

In 1970, well after the bombing halt had gone into effect, the "protective reaction strike" emerged as a new tactic. Despite the nebulous understanding between Henry Kissinger and the North Vietnamese delegation in Paris, unarmed reconnaissance flights were regularly fired upon over the North. Consequently, a policy emerged in TF 77 which allowed retaliation against NVN defenses when fired upon. Later this

policy was amended to permit preemption if fire control
radar locked onto U.S. aircraft. Immediately after the
1968 bombing halt, most photo recon flights were
conducted south of the 20th Parallel near the Laotian
passes where supplies passed along the Ho Chi Minh
Trail. And if there just happened to be a mini-Alpha in
the area when the bad guys started shooting, well, the
coincidence was deemed fortuitous by the photo pilots.

Another reason for stand-downs, rarely if ever admitted at the time, was visiting antiwar delegations
from the U.S. The most publicized were trips by actress
Jane Fonda and former Attorney General Ramsey Clark,
but other individuals and groups, such as the Friends'
"peace boat" that brought food and medical supplies,
were occasionally responsible for postponing air ops.
Usually the white three-masted schooner, crewed and
funded by Quakers, would bring a halt to strikes around
Haiphong. Apparently Washington was concerned with
these people's safety—a concern seldom shared at air
wing level.

It's interesting to speculate upon the long-term
effects had Fonda, Clark, and the Friends established
residence in Hanoi and Haiphong. Would their continued presence have brought a halt to all bombing of
those areas? A hypothetical question, for there were no
film producers in Hanoi, and the amenities of Haiphong
lacked a good deal in comparison to Washington's gilded ambience, let alone that of Hollywood.

Stand-downs Up North invariably brought about a
resumption of strikes into Laos. Operation Steel Tiger
lasted almost as long as Rolling Thunder, but officially it
never existed. We were firmly and repeatedly instructed never to discuss Steel Tiger with anyone, and if
questioned directly, to deny its existence.

TF 77 flew Steel Tiger strikes about as often as
Alphas. The usual route in was over South Vietnam,
returning to Dixie Station the same way. But despite its

"secret" nature, Steel Tiger had its own peculiar ROE. In deference to Laotian authority, no ordnance could be dropped unless authorized by a Laotian forward air controller.

The Laotian Air Force had precious few pilots to spare for such duty. And coordination and liaison with U.S. Air Force or Navy units was frequently complicated by the language barrier. So the sports down in the squadrons found expedient alternatives to getting on with the war.

We'll never know how many times some unsuspecting Laotian GI was summarily scooped up, strapped into a T-28's back seat, and taken for an airplane ride. He probably wasn't a pilot, may not have even spoken English, but by God he was wearing a Laotian uniform and he was airborne in the FAC plane when the strike birds arrived. "Congratulations, Nim, you are now a forward air controller. Enjoy the view." Actually, the view was often spectacular and richly contradictory. The beauty of the lush green jungle was contrasted by eruptions of orange napalm or the unforgettable white tendrils of phosphorus bombs.

But from the fighter-bomber pilot's viewpoint, that was about all that Steel Tiger had to offer: scenery. There wasn't much satisfaction in dropping ordnance in the jungle because the only aiming point was the FAC's smoke rocket. Aviators seldom knew what good they'd done, for the target was hidden from view.

Many times there wasn't even an opportunity to drop ordnance. If the FAC had departed, it was standard operating procedure to reverse course and head for the boat. Anything could have happened: the FAC might have sustained battle damage or run low on fuel. The best the strike birds could hope for was diversion to a convenient FAC in South Vietnam before reaching "bingo" fuel.

Another peculiarity of Steel Tiger concerned some

early escape and evasion briefings. Various spooks, some-times from State and sometimes from CIA, told air-crews they should regard Laotian troops encountered after bailout as friendly. This was, to understate mat-ters, an opinion based upon supreme optimism.

The first navy aircraft shot down in Indochina was a VFP-63 RF-8 in May 1964. That was three months before the Gulf of Tonkin incident.

The pilot of the photo Crusader ejected and was captured by Pathet Lao troops—friends of the folks who'd shot him down in the first place. After about two weeks the flier managed to escape and, happily, returned to safety. But how anyone could expect aviators to consider *any* uniformed troops as friendly eludes expla-nation even two decades later.

Thus far we've dealt solely with the political factors of ROE. Nevertheless, there are a couple of areas over which the navy did have some control. The first was hung bombs. The shackles and multiple-ejector racks occasionally malfunctioned, as any device will. When that happened, only God and Sir Isaac Newton had any idea where the ordnance was going. Sometimes it was going into a residential neighborhood in downtown Hanoi, sometimes very close to a Russian ship in Haiphong Harbor. In either case, the opposition never missed a chance to wail loud and long about "indiscrim-inate terror bombing."

The first such cries I remember hearing of came in 1966. The issue received wide play when *New York Times* correspondent Harrison Salisbury was invited to Hanoi to survey things. His reports on damage to civilian areas directly contradicted LBJ's oft-avowed opinion that the U.S. was conducting a surgical bombing campaign in scrupulous observance of civilian and neu-tral rights.

The military dropped the ball here on two points.

First, the Joint Chiefs failed to impress upon Johnson that "surgical bombing" is possible only when the threat level, aviator skill, and mechanical reliability all pull together. Any one of those factors can easily upset the equation.

Second, neither the navy nor the air force ever went public with what some would call an admission, what others would call a simple fact: Murphy's Law is always in effect. Whether from political considerations from DOD or the Oval Office, or from an unwillingness to appear less than perfect, senior airmen would rarely address the subject of malfunctions resulting in civilian deaths or damage. In the arena of public opinion, it was a serious omission.

In the end, all the fuss and bother about ROE came down to a ten-word distillation from the most successful general of both Indochina wars. Vo Nguyen Giap, interviewed in 1982, concluded, "There is only one rule in war: one must win."[7]

Strike it in bronze.

3

MORALE: THE ONLY WAR WE HAD

> *I doubt if Mr. McNamara and his crew have any morale setting on their computers.*
>
> —*Rear Admiral D. V. Gallery*
> *1965*

When the *Ticonderoga* sailed for the western Pacific in 1966, one of her F-8 pilots was left on the dock. He lacked just a few more flights in the replacement squadron before joining Air Wing 19, but he had to stand there, watching his departing friends through tear-blurred eyes. It was a heart-wrenching sight: an accomplished, aggressive aviator in tears because he was missing the war.

Six years later the *Hancock* departed Alameda as the last *Essex*-class carrier headed for the Tonkin Gulf. At 0800, approaching the Golden Gate Bridge, the skipper ordered general quarters. Sailors could see traffic backed up for miles, the bridge being kept clear lest protesters drop explosives on the flight deck. A squadron commander who had flown from *Tico* in '66 stalked down to his room, threw himself on his bunk, and cried.

Between those two tearful departures lay the story

of morale in naval aviation from 1965 to 1973. Napoleon observed, "In war, everything depends on morale; and morale and public opinion comprise the better part of reality." He could have been speaking about Vietnam.

Aviators' attitudes passed through four identifiable stages. Phase One lasted about four years, from 1964 through 1968 and perhaps into 1969. Morale was high and declined only slightly during this period. The majority of aviators were pumped full of the Right Stuff: cocky, aggressive, and proud. Few were anxious to go to war but they shared the attitude of the fireman who said, "I don't want there to be a fire, but if there is one, I hope the alarm rings while I'm on duty." There were several reasons for the high state of morale. Professionalism was a dominant motivation. We had accepted the king's shilling for years, and now we were expected to pay back the investment. It was not only expected of us; we expected it of ourselves.

Another motivating concept was the idea of military flying as a vocation. Lieutenants and lieutenant commanders particularly held this attitude. Our entire working lives had been spent in preparation for combat. Now that war had begun, our skills were in demand. How well had we in fact prepared ourselves?

The basic motivation was pride, though that's a charitable way to phrase it. Thomas Wolfe wrote that surgeons are hard to beat for egotism but fighter pilots come close. (Maybe he doesn't know enough fighter pilots.) Pride and its first cousins, self-respect and ego, had a lot to do with motivation. At one level, tactical aviators wondered self-consciously if they really were as good as they told one another. An on another level, they wondered if they were as brave as they made out. They knew time would tell.

The aviators headed for combat in the mid-1960s shared common characteristics. All were well educated, some with advanced degrees, and most were stable family men with career goals. Some could be described as cerebral, and there was a sprinkling of genuine philosophers. In contrast, yet somehow completely melded, was the fighter jock mentality. But make no mistake about it, many carrier-based attack pilots had the VF attitude just as much as the Phantom and Crusader drivers.

Hard-core aviators would rather die than look bad. They would shun the adage "death before dishonor" as pretentious, but that's exactly what many believe. One of the better-known characters in the Crusader community intentionally rode a spinning F-8 down to the wave-tops rather than eject and have the boys say, "Old Norm couldn't hack the program." Well, Old Norm *did* hack the program, but he almost died in the process. There were others just like him.

There were also some officers, including a few outstanding stick-and-rudder men, who felt few of these motivations. They were simply careerists who wanted their tickets punched along the way. And one of the stops on the road to rear admiral was a combat tour.

Others, fewer yet, never made a WestPac deployment. Sometimes wives dug in their heels and, in effect, said, "me or the war. Take your pick." This situation wasn't as noteworthy as the fact that a fleet aviator could elude combat for as much as eight years. For an airman enjoys a luxury which the infantryman never knows. It's the easiest thing in the world to get grounded temporarily or removed from flight status entirely. And it needn't be anything so dramatic as marching into the CO's office and dropping your wings on the desk. All it took was the merest hint that flying had lost some of its appeal. A casual remark at the O Club or a couple of aborted flights on marginal grounds seldom went unnoticed. Little things like that, coupled with a confirming remark, were all anyone required. You were still in the navy, but out of the war. And out of contention.

Actually, the men who turned in their wings were appreciated by those who kept flying. Nobody wanted to go over the beach with someone whose heart wasn't in his work. Far better to 'fess up and make room for somebody with tiger blood in his veins.

Two incidents from 1968 illustrate the state of aviator morale in Task Force 77; one humorous in retrospect, the other as serious as a heart attack.

The Department of Defense sent a team of medical researchers to Yankee Station, intent upon discovering how aviators reacted to various stress levels. The medicos were greeted by the fliers with something short of unbridled enthusiasm. But finally twenty pilots agreed to be wired with sensors that monitored physiological functions: respiration, heart rate, and so forth.

After the data were compiled, the doctors scratched their heads and pondered the contradiction staring back from their charts. They discovered to their surprise that the "test subjects" had reacted to stress in the inverse order from what the doctors had predicted. The medics, lacking any flying experience, noted with alarm that an aviator's vital signs showed twice the stress calling the ball in a night carrier landing as over downtown Hanoi in broad daylight.

Actually, jinking through AAA and dodging SAMs ranked only third in stress level. It was far behind a nocturnal carrier landing and still quite a way below the adrenaline quotient of a night catapult shot. All DOD had to do to arrive at the same data was to talk to any group of naval aviators, who would have told them where the thrill was for half the cost.

A sterner test of Phase One morale occurred during the first half of March 1968. Following the North

Korea's seizure of the USS *Pueblo*, two carriers with their screens were sent far north to the Sea of Japan. A contingency plan was invoked that committed the *Enterprise* and *Ticonderoga* to launch air strikes against North Korean airfields.

Air Force planes in South Korea were to have coordinated with the two navy air wings, but it was still a vastly lopsided proposition. The carriers were assigned seven airfields at which were based more than two hundred MiGs. Intelligence briefings detailed the enemy order of battle: ninety-one MiG-21s, seventy-six MiG-17s, and thirty-five MiG-19s. It was estimated that at least half the North Korean fighter force would be airborne by the time the strikes arrived. Against this, we had twenty operational Phantoms and eighteen Crusaders to escort the strike birds.

The fighters were spread mighty thin. One target was to be struck by ten A-4s escorted by a pair of F-8s.

Nobody slept much that night. A good many farewell letters were written in expectation of the worst, though "the worst" varied from one man to another, according to his outlook. If forced down alive, the pilots knew they faced brutal captivity in a land ruled by barbarians. A safe bailout into the sea was only marginally more attractive—the water was studded with ice, and even in "poopy suits" survival would be measured in minutes.

Yet nobody backed out. Launch was scheduled for 0600, and at 0430 aircrews were suiting up or eating breakfast. The briefings had been grim. There was absolutely no joking. But sometime before 0500 word came through that the mission was scrubbed. It was never known if political considerations swayed the decision makers in Washington, or if military reality forced itself upon them. In either case, two air wings heaved a collective sigh of relief.[1]

But the point worth making is that morale held. Knowing the odds against returning were extremely slim, every pilot assigned to the strike would have manned his airplane and launched. They would have rather died than looked bad.

Phase Two began sometime in 1969, after Lyndon Johnson's bombing halt of November 1968. By then, an unspoken frustration had crept into squadron ready rooms. As if by tacit agreement the emphasis switched from purely mission-oriented considerations to one of mutual care and concern. With no stated goal in sight from the national leadership, and no end in sight to the war, aviators began to adopt an attitude best expressed as "Let's watch out for each other."

This is not to say that Task Force 77 became any less interested in doing the job. Nobody ever heard the attack pilots say, "Let's pull out at 5,000 instead of 3,000." Nobody heard of anti-SAM Iron Hands or flak suppressors taking any less interest. But there was a new sense of awareness that the politicians didn't quite know what to do with us, so we'd have to look out for ourselves.

Previously, ships' libraries seldom did much business in books about Indochina. But by 1969 or 1970 it was almost impossible to find such volumes on the shelves. There were long waiting lists as more people began questioning the origins of the war, seeking information to form their own opinions. Accepted premises about nation building came in for close scrutiny, and some began to wonder if South Vietnam would ever become a nation in its own right.

My own conviction that we faced a morale crisis occurred—I hesitate to use the phrase—on a dark and stormy night in February 1968. My wingman and I were scheduled for a night BarCAP from the *Ticonderoga* at 2145 hours on the sixth. The weather was very poor, with rain and a low overcast. It wasn't a cheery mission for a new young pilot, but my wingman, Wendell Brown, was up to the task.

The two-hour mission was uneventful, and we returned for a carrier-controlled approach (CCA). We had been refueled on station and began our approach with a maximum amount of landing fuel, 2,500 pounds. This was the first time in my flying life that I had made a CCA without breaking out of the overcast by minimum altitude. I was well below 200 feet when waved off over a blur of light (the landing signal mirror). I climbed back to 2,000 feet. I was then notified that my wingman had also been waved off, and we were directed to tank from the airborne KA-3. Wendell and I joined up and met the tanker at 20,000 feet over the ship.

Our fuel state was about 1,200 pounds each. I plugged into the KA-3 and took 3,000 pounds. Brown lined up and began to stab at the basket. It was perhaps more difficult to plug in an F-8 than any other airplane because the probe is mounted portside at shoulder level. Trying to eyeball it doesn't work; all you can do is just line up near the basket and close in until you feel contact. Then you look to see if your probe is connected. If you fence with it, the task becomes almost impossible. After six or seven stabs, Wendell hit the basket's lip at a substantial closure rate. His probe caved in the basket and it began to sway laterally, making contact impossible.

Wendell's fuel was down to 500 pounds, and the ship was frantic. The *Tico* launched an A-4 with "buddy pack" refueling tanks, and we joined on it. Wendell was down to 200 pounds. I was coaching him just as I did students in the replacement squadron.

"Now just settle down. Take your time. Position yourself and drive it home!" We held our collective

Douglas A-3 Skywarrior

breath; he was down to zero as he closed on the basket.

Direct hit! Beautiful. I shouted, "You got it, push it in!" There wasn't one second to spare. The tankers green light came on, indicating the F-8's probe was in far enough to receive fuel. I fairly shouted at the A-4, "Pump him some gas!"

We watched as the hose withdrew from Wendell's probe and slammed back inside the tanker package. There was an almost audible gasp.

The A-4 tanker pilot has several switches on his console. The "Transfer Fuel" switch is next to the "Retract Hose" switch, and you know which one was used.

I screamed, Wendell Brown screamed, the ship screamed, and I suppose the tanker pilot screamed. The hose came back out immediately and Wendell maneuvered into position for a last try. Then his engine quit. He was out of fuel.

We descended together back into the overcast, and Wendell ejected at 10,000 feet. Helicopters couldn't locate him in the thick weather. That was bad enough, but then I had to worry about my own situation.

The ship told me the "bingo" airfield was Da Nang. I got to Da Nang all right, but as I passed the threshold prior to touchdown I was greeted by a stream of tracers. The base was under attack—it was Tet, 1968.

I'd been airborne 2.7 hours, with one hour in the airplane before launch. It was now almost 0100 as I taxied to a stop near the tower. The thump of shellfire came to me as I climbed down from the cockpit.

Entering the operations office, I asked if there were any word on my wingman. Nobody knew anything about him. I took off my G-suit and harness and lay down on the floor. It felt good to stretch out, and I was content to stay there until morning. Things couldn't get much worse. This was already the worst night of my life.

Within minutes a rough hand shook me awake. I looked up at an air force colonel, who was wide-eyed and frantic. He asked, "Is that your aircraft out front?" It was. "You have to get it out of here. I have no revetment for it. It must get out of here."

My next response was profane. Then I said, "If you want it moved, move it yourself."

The colonel became irrational. He said, "I will bulldoze it off the ramp if you don't get it off the field." At first I thought he was blustering, maybe resentful of a navy type taking up USAF ramp space. But I looked closer and realized I was dealing with a madman. He had become unglued.

"Where the hell can I go?" I asked. "The ship can't take me. The weather is terrible all over Indochina."

"I don't give a damn," he retorted. "Just get it out of here." There was no choice. I knew beyond doubt that this near-hysterical man, completely demoralized, would bulldoze my beautiful fighter into a pile of scrap. I suited up and launched for Sangley Point about 0300, flying eight hundred miles across the South China Sea.

Two hours later, with the sun rising in front of me, I landed in the Philippines. No wallet, no money, just my Geneva Convention ID card. I sent a message to the *Tico*, which soon drew a response: "You're where?"

Upon return to the ship on the eighth I was debriefed by the CarDiv commander, who sent some one to Da Nang. The end result was the air force colonel went home early. The only good news was that Wendell Brown was picked up the following day, after two and a half days in the water. But from that time on, it became apparent that the war was exacting an undue price in American morale.

Over the next couple of years, more third- and fourth-tour pilots showed up. Quite simply, we were short of aviators willing to make repeated combat tours. After three WestPac deployments most fliers felt they'd earned a rest, and justifiably so. This attitude, coupled with a normal desire for career-enhancing slots such as attaches or postgraduate study, meant a drain upon the aviator pool.

Pilots' relationships with their detailers occasionally took sharp turns. A flier with multiple combat cruises, or a flier determined to avoid the first such cruise, had different ways of going about his next assignment. He might say, "You know, I've been flying A-4s for six years now. I'd sort of like to move up. How about a transition to A-6s?" The pilot knew, and the detailer knew, that such a change would remove the aviator from combat for a year and a half or more. So would a posting to a language school or a staff desk.

Previously, that same aviator might have drawn a slot in Training Command, and he'd have howled a dirge of insult and lament. "Training Command? You kidding? Ain't no war in Corpus Christi. Get me a slot in AirPac so I can log some combat!"

In truth, if a flier wanted combat, he could get it.

Officially, he could wave his orders aloft and bemoan the fate which sent him to attache duty in London or CinCPac Fleet in Hawaii, but that was strictly for show. There was never a detailer behind a desk who refused to send a flier to a westbound fleet squadron.

Phase Three of the morale situation began with the mining of Haiphong in May 1972. Spirits took an immediate upturn. We felt as though we were finally at war. More lucrative targets were opening up almost daily after four dreary years. The Hanoi-Haiphong causeway, hydroelectric plants, serious stuff. Pilots clamored for juicy strikes, actually argued about who had flown the previous Iron Hand, and began counting MiG kills. It was good to see progress. Maybe the end was in sight.

The fighter and attack pilots took a bit of an insult as a result of the mining success. Lloyds of London issued a worldwide notice that insurance was canceled for any ship entering the mine zone. Dozens of vessels were caught inside Haiphong harbor, no supplies were moving, and things were suddenly looking up. It was demeaning to think of those passive AWT-1 gadgets lurking in the coastal waterways, doing overnight what years of intense strike warfare hadn't. Of course, in all that time we'd been sent after bicycle factories and the like. But still it rankled. Aviators' egos are easily bruised.

In under eight months the war Up North had turned around. Fleet aviators saw the dramatic change on every trip over the beach. SAMs became almost nonexistent, and AAA dribbled off from 85mm barrages to a token squirt here and there of 23- or maybe 37mm. Few supplies were getting in. Little was moving on the ground, for bridges and rail lines were shattered. When Air Force F-4s finally toppled Thanh Hoa Bridge with smart bombs, we knew we had it knocked.

After yet another olive-branch bombing halt, North Vietnamese intransigence in Paris increased. The

SAM

eleven-day "Christmas War" that followed convinced
Hanoi that it was better to bargain, and the air war
entered its fourth and final stage. For lack of a better
term, we might say it was characterized by The Last
Man Syndrome.

Nobody wanted to be the last to die in a winless
war. For that matter, nobody wanted to be next-to-last,
either. But there was a distinct change in attitude from
Phase Two in which the watchword was mutual protection: "Let's take care of each other." Now in many cases
it was, "I'm taking care of *me*." And it wasn't tacit
anymore. It turned vocal. Quiet, self-conscious young
aviators who had seldom said a word in briefing now
watched operations officers chalk up names for dicey
targets and immediately shouted, "Hey, wait a minute.
I had a flak suppressor yesterday. It's not my turn!"

This breach of ready room decorum was astonishing.
Such an outburst came from the same sort of pilot who
had previously believed it was better to die than to look

bad. And the curious thing was that his chances of survival were vastly greater than before, because the level of threat had diminished. This same flier would have moaned on an earlier cruise about "another goddam BarCAP," famous for lack of action. Now he cherished the assignment.

Squadron commanders went through hell during this period. They felt the same emotions as their pilots, but had to maintain the facade of the gung-ho aviator. (It's better to die than look bad.) Reluctant to speak of the problem at first, many COs tried to deal with it themselves, wondering how their leadership had failed.

In truth, almost every squadron CO had similar problems. Only later, when air wing commanders began holding informal meetings with squadron COs and execs, did we realize that everybody faced the same problem.

Leadership became more important than ever. Squadron commanders and division leaders had to fly every rugged mission. "Bad places, good targets" was how they expressed it. Ops officers had to be meticulously careful in rotating sporty assignments, and they were bending over backwards to be fair. But still some arguments arose.

At least when words were exchanged it helped clear the air. When aircraft "problems" arose, it was much tougher. Some pilots reported mysterious glitches that were never diagnosed by the plane captains and mechanics. Radio failure was another way out. All it took was a thumb on the microphone button immediately after turning on the set. Without time to warm up, keying the mike would pop the circuit breaker and the bird was "down" for that hop.

This reluctance was not peculiar to Vietnam, nor was it of epidemic proportions. It's likely to happen at the end of every war. But some aspects of Nam made morale droop lower than it did at the end of other wars. One report making the intelligence rounds was that the opposition had stopped taking prisoners. The Viet Cong were always disinclined to capture people, if for no other reason than logistics. And the NVA became that way. They had all the POWs they needed, so what difference did a few murders make to them?

The POW/MIA situation affected morale almost from the beginning. Wives of MIA airmen lived in limbo, some for as long as seven years, even when eyewitness reports made it plain the missing man was most likely dead. Perhaps the navy in an effort to be kind had done more harm than good.

True, there were instances where aviators miraculously survived. But these few examples fueled false hopes in most cases. The navy probably would have done better to present the facts and report its reasonable conclusion that the airman was dead.

In large part, the confusion and pain was a product of the enemy's calculated policy of noncooperation. For the third time in recent history, we found ourselves engaged against an Asian opponent who refused to provide an thorough accounting of POWs. The North Vietnamese knew how important the issue was to the American public, and they exploited the situation.

The women left behind at Miramar or Lemoore— "cruise widows"—had their own effect on morale. It was tough enough on a CO's wife to deal with the inevitable nocturnal phone calls from the Bureau of Personnel, tougher still to maintain the spirits of those whose husbands were still flying.

Around 1967, navy men and women began asking questions—hard questions—of civilian authorities. Why were not the Swiss or the Red Cross reporting on the status of POWs in North Vietnam? Why didn't the U.S. government exert its influence with those agencies to obtain information on who was and was not held Up North? After all, was not Hanoi a signatory to the 1954 Geneva Accords?

No satisfactory answers were forthcoming. There were references to "delicate negotiations" and "ongoing efforts," but in the end it amounted to a smokescreen. The U.S. government simply failed in its responsibility to the MIA families, who finally formed their own organization. They, unlike a good many diplomats, were unconcerned with "upsetting" Hanoi over this issue.[2]

The military put a great deal of effort into preventing POW/MIA situations from arising through its work in search and rescue (SAR). We got off to a slow, shaky start in combat SAR, but progress was made, and seldom was effort spared to retrieve downed fliers as long as a reasonable chance of their survival remained.

Cost-analysis devotees during the McNamara years occasionally pointed out the financial discrepancy in risking even low-priced assets such as H-2s and A-1s in rescue attempts. After all they calculated, there were always more aviators than airplanes, so why expose additional aircraft and crews to increased risk just to fetch back one flier who got himself bagged?[3]

Of course, if someone had to ask such a question, that person wouldn't understand the answer anyway. As Dan Gallery said, "I doubt if Mr. McNamara and his crew have any morale setting on their computers." And Cap'n Dan was exactly right. There was no way to quantify the morale of aviators who flew over the beach in total confidence that choppers, "Spads," and ResCAP birds were waiting just offstage. There was no better support than *knowing* that if *you* got in a little trouble, friends would be there.

Later in the war navy fliers received cheerful news when they learned that air force helos were operating Up North. These were the "Jolly Green Giants," flown

"Jolly Green Giant"

by men of incredible courage. They'd set down inside North Vietnam, monitoring strike frequency in case somebody had to eject. Operating farther inland than TF 77 helos could go, the Jollies provided magnificent service to air force and navy aircrews alike.

The SAR crews won not only the undying gratitude of rescued aviators but also a lot of decorations, a further indication—if one is needed—of the danger of their job. The crews of HC-7, who performed most of the navy's combat SAR throughout the war, collectively won a Medal of Honor, four Navy Crosses, numerous Silver Stars, and more than fifty Distinguished Flying Crosses. Another Medal of Honor went to a Marine Corps helo pilot for a combat rescue over land.

But ironically, as with so much connected with the Vietnam War, medals eventually produced results contrary to their intended purpose. Because awards were made almost on a production-line basis, the value of a decoration declined. In a war where computer programmers received Bronze Stars, other decorations—bravely earned—were diminished by comparison. So many sorties for an Air Medal, certain results for a

DFC; a Silver Star for a MiG kill. The latter rankled some hardcore fighter pilots. After all, how many fliers in World War II received that decoration for shooting down one airplane? If a medal is going to be worn with pride, it must be awarded as an exception, not as a rule.

Thus far we've concentrated upon the morale of aviators. But on a carrier there were one hundred twenty-five pilots supported by perhaps five thousand enlisted men. The working hours and conditions under which those youngsters labored—many of them less than twenty years of age—tested many stout hearts.

Mechanics, plane handlers, catapult crews, and others worked extremely hard. Frequently they would be so tired they would simply flop down on the deck or crawl into a corner to catch some much-needed sleep. Carriers are noisy, crowded places to work at the best of times. In war, with strikes launching and recovering and ordnance being handled and loaded constantly, the pressure of the pace is enormous. Perhaps the biggest boost to these kids' morale would have been some of their own kind—enlisted troopers—flying combat. That's not as contradictory as it sounds. The young sailors loading ordnance or fueling aircraft had no real frame of reference, little sense of identification, with what happened between launch and recovery. Once in a while there might be some excitement if a fighter pilot bagged a MiG with a Sidewinder some kid had loaded on his airplane, but otherwise it was hard, unglamorous work.

But imagine if an aviation technician rode the back seat of an F-4 or monitored the scope in an A-6. He'd come back full of tales about what he'd seen and done over the beach. He could provide his friends with a firsthand sense of contribution to the effort.

Another big factor in morale was shore leave.

Three main liberty ports were available to TF 77: Subic Bay in the Philippines, Singapore, or Hong Kong. The enlisted folks dearly loved Olongapo, north of Subic Bay. The storied pleasures of Po City were far beyond its actual offerings, but the ridiculously low prices for all manner of carnal indulgence made that pest-ridden mudhole a magnet for sailors. Everything there was cheap: booze, floozies, and room and board.

Some bizarre stories emanated from Olongapo. In 1972, when Ferdinand Marcos declared martial law, he cracked down on drug abuse. Executions were not unusual for smugglers and dealers. Sailors returning to duty had tales of awakening to gunfire several mornings in a row. Cocking a bleary eye at his watch, a seaman might mutter, "Hmmm. Firing squad's a little late this morning." Then he'd roll over and go back to sleep.

For the aviators, Subic had rather less exotic attractions. There were two officers' clubs, but only one where the birdmen could flock together. On the Subic side was a fine facility with formal dining, a nice dance floor—all the trappings. It was mainly patronized by the naval base personnel, refined individuals who pulled out their ladies' chairs when seating them, and generally behaved as Congress intended for officers and gentlemen.

On the Cubi Point side, at the air station, was "the zoo." With the war on and all, there evolved a grudging tolerance for the antics that characterized the Cubi Point O Club. As long as the animals remained in the zoo, they were pretty much on their own.

The Cubi club assumed the atmosphere of a third-rate bistro. Worn-out furniture was *de rigueur,* not because of monetary problems, but because of the imaginative uses to which it was subjected. Aviators stacked chairs and tables to the ceiling, vying with one another to see who could build the tallest pile. There

were food fights and fist fights. Pilots took the microphone from the Filipino singers and showed the local
talent how it was done. The hoarse shouting that passed
for singing among aviators had to be heard to be
believed.

Closing time was officially 0100. Not that it mattered
much. When the Filipino proprietor optimistically announced, "Time for one more drink before closing," he
may or may not have been heeded. Often as not, some
tipsy aviator swayed on the stage, announcing, "No way,
Jose. This joint closes when we leave."

On occasion that was the air wing commander.

If the officer of the day was so insensitive as to
attempt to enforce the local ordinance, he might find
himself bound and gagged behind the bar. Not out of
malevolence, you understand; merely in the interest of
continuing the evening's entertainment.

A law of nature holds that alcohol fuels all wars.
And the lads at Cubi never suffered a fuel crisis. They
got knee-walking, commode-hugging drunk the first
couple of days, then recuperated with golf, swimming,
or deep breathing. After a while the base commander
realized he needed to lure the troops from the bar. So
he gave the boys a toy.

It was an inspired decision. A length of track was
laid from the edge of the pond back to a specially built
shed. The shed housed a hydraulic catapult that propelled an F-8 nose section down the track at dizzying
speed. The cockpit was fully equipped with flight controls and throttle (none of which exerted any control
over the gadget's trajectory) and an arresting hook.

The object of the game was to drop the hook at the
exact split-second the hurtling cockpit passed over a
four-foot section of track equipped with arresting wires.
Drop the hook too early and it skipped over the wires.
Too late and you missed the wires entirely. In either

case, you bolstered directly into the slimy pool. To make a successful "landing" took a keen eye and a steady hand, neither of which was likely to characterize the occupant.

Inside the shed were hundreds of autographs. Every optimistic fool who ever rode that battered Crusader scrawled his or her name on the wall. It would be interesting to know what became of the contraption.

Maybe they put it in storage for next time.

4

THE SURFACE THREAT: AAA AND SAMS

They talked about shooting down American planes with a sort of childlike wonder about why the pilots kept flying into their flak and SAMs. There was admiration in their voices, but pity, too.

—William Broyles, Jr.
"A Veteran's Return to Vietnam"
The Atlantic, *April 1985*

The Cuban situation of 1962–64 produced a handful of incidents that bore a disproportionate influence upon tactical air doctrine for the next several years. Most of the naval aviators flying Up North from 1965 through 1968 were products of those early Cuban years. Although a few MiGs were encountered at odd intervals and Soviet surface-to-air missiles had knocked down high-flying U-2s at least twice, the greatest threat to planes was actually posed by guns. And we had lost sight of that. We had lost sight of that because we had lost our institutional memory. Somewhere in the Navy Department's archives was a series of War College studies, circa 1954–56, that evaluated aircraft losses in

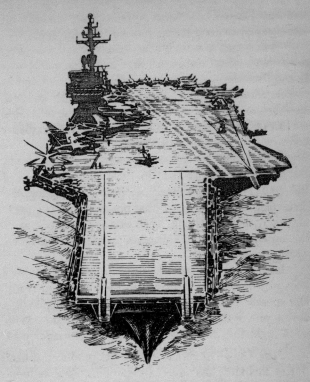

U.S.S. Kitty Hawk

Korea.[1] Some 540 Navy and Marine Corps tactical aircraft had fallen to enemy gunfire during that war, and that fact should have told us something. Nevertheless, the conventional wisdom maintained that space-age missiles were the primary threat. It had to be the case; everybody said so.

Had they taken time to check the boxscore, the whiz kids in the Pentagon would have found that more than seventy Navy and Marine Corps jet aircraft were knocked down by communist gunners.[2] Nobody had told the Chinese or North Koreans they couldn't hit fast-movers, so they had gotten on with the war.

The secret was really no secret at all. Gunners didn't have to track a jet. All they had to do was draw a straight line between the airplane's roll-in point and its target, then fill that portion of the sky with as much steel as possible. Regardless of its speed, the jet had to fly through that box. At that point, probability theory takes over. It becomes a crapshoot.

Yet this fact of elementary gunnery eluded us. In the dozen years from 1953 to 1965, the emergence of the SAM threat distracted us from recognizing the danger of AAA. Convinced that practice bombing techniques with low-altitude, shallow-angle delivery were the answer, we found ourselves suddenly confronted with a sky full of flak.

Lieutenant Chuck Klussman in May 1964 over Laos was one of the first to learn the unpleasant truth. His speedy RF-8 was hit hard by Laotian 37mm fire during one of the first Yankee Team recon flights. With an in-flight fire, he nursed his crippled Crusader back to the *Kitty Hawk* and landed safely aboard. But a couple of weeks later, on 6 June, the Laotian gunners got his range again and this time they shot him down. Fortunately, the VFP-63 pilot escaped from what could have been long-term or permanent captivity. But it should have been obvious to one and all that fast jets weren't invulnerable to gunfire.

Three months later we ran up against communist AAA gunners again. Of sixty-four sorties flown against North Vietnamese PT-boat bases in Operation Pierce Arrow we lost two planes. One was destroyed outright and the other was badly damaged. One pilot, Lieutenant (jg) Richard Sather, was killed and the other, Lieutenant (jg) Everett Alvarez, ejected from his stricken A-4C to become shootdown number one, beginning an eight-year stint as a POW. It was to be a period of horrendous aircraft losses.

Through March 1965, when Rolling Thunder began, the navy's attrition fluctuated between fifteen and thirty losses per one thousand sorties. To put that figure in perspective, the absolute highest loss rate for the rest of the war was barely seven per thousand, and that came in late 1965 and early 1966 when we went into Route Pack VI in a big way. From mid-1966 on, the attrition over the North never reached *four* per thousand.[3]

How can the drastic difference be explained? It's simple: low-level attacks with treetop pullouts put aircraft within range not only of AAA but of smallarms as well. And barrage fire worked just fine, even with the relatively limited number of antiaircraft guns available at the time. In early 1965 the North Vietnamese had barely one thousand medium- and heavy-caliber guns: 37-, 57-, 85-, and 100mm. By late summer the number had tripled, and by the end of 1966 there were between six thousand and seven thousand guns Up North of greater than 20mm.

Few of these guns were radar-controlled, but they didn't have to be. The light-caliber weapons were mobile and could be towed to new sites easily. Pure concentration was the name of the game—concentration and fire discipline.

Originally most of the AAA crews were "volunteers" from either the Chinese army or air force. Undoubtedly many of them benefitted from experience in Korea. But they passed on their knowledge and doctrine to the Vietnamese. Servicing an artillery piece, regardless of its target, is almost a mechanical procedure. It requires a good deal of coordination among the guncrew members for maximum efficiency, but the skills required are elementary. With practice, the efficiency level is easily maintained.

The enemy gunners Up North were disciplined and courageous. If ordered to fire at a specific sector of sky, they did so regardless of our flak suppressors, even if the jets attacked from another angel. The crews relied upon their comrades in other batteries to cover them, and if those folks missed—well, there were more trainees available.

The North Vietnamese perfected the antiaircraft gunner's art, although in truth it was more science than art. It was possible to mathematically compute the amount of explosives per second required in a column of air to render an object flying through that column statistically vulnerable. The communists' sector-fire technique was excellent, and they could fill a five-square-mile column with murderous flak from 3,000 to 20,000 feet.

It was awesome, it was spectacular, it was perilously close to beautiful. The light guns, 23- and 37mm, burst with white smoke. The 57mm shells exploded in dark gray and the heavy 85- and 100mm stuff erupted in black clouds. Mix in occasional strings of colored tracer from heavy machine guns arcing up to perhaps 5,000 feet, and you can imagine all these varicolored clouds bursting somewhere in that cone of air every second for several minutes.

A French journalist came out to the *Hancock* during her 1968 cruise and told the aviators what he'd seen and heard during a strike at Hanoi a couple of weeks before. First came the warning sirens and a hasty but orderly rush to the air-raid shelters. In a few minutes people on the ground could hear the approaching jets, and almost immediately the guns crashed into action.

It wasn't a stuttering, tentative rumble that built to a mighty crescendo. Quite the contrary. Every gun ordered to fire opened up at the same second, and the shooting remained at that peak intensity for the duration of the raid. The noise was indescribable, and at time the shock, concussion, and vibration seemed unbearable.

If the target was nearby, residents might hear or feel the bombs exploding, and they might detect the screech of jets pulling off the target. Then the shooting stopped, as if a conductor had slashed down his baton.

Thinking little of the aftermath, the reporter said he stood up and took a step toward the exit of the shelter. But his North Vietnamese guide grabbed him by the arm. Pointing to his watch, the officer said, "We must wait."

Uncertain of the reason for the delay, the journalist sat down again, noting that everyone else in the shelter also seemed content to wait. Within several seconds he became aware of a tinkling sound outside. Slowly the sound grew to a constant pattering in the street, lasting perhaps three minutes.

By then our friendly Frenchman had figured it out. Shell fragments and splinters were falling over the area. Many had tumbled down from 20,000 feet, and it took them that long to fall. When he emerged from the bunker, he saw the street and sidewalk littered with shiny, minute pieces of metal that formed a gray coating on all surfaces.

That was an air raid from the groundling's viewpoint.

It was decidedly different from the cockpit of a fighter-bomber. There was no way to defeat barrage fire. Pilots could dodge and jink to evade aimed fire, but in a dive through a sector filled with smoking, crackling flak there was no point. Some aviators jinked anyway, just to keep up their morale, but many squadron commanders laid down the law: no jinking. Concentrate on your dive, placing the piper where it belongs and putting your ordnance on the target. That's why you flew all that way, so make your sortie count.

The latter was the professionally correct approach. It didn't take an accountant to figure that in a piece of sky filled with barrage fire, a plane was just as likely to get hit while indulging in world-class jinking as when flying straight and level.

Airplanes aren't meant to duel with guns; that is now doctrine at Naval Strike Warfare Center. Smallarms and AAA accounted for by far the greatest portion of in-flight losses during the Vietnam War. Among navy aircraft, losses to gunfire amounted to 58 percent of total losses on combat missions, including 77 percent of shootdowns in cases where the cause was known. One quarter of the losses were unattributable to either combat or operational causes; many planes launched and simply were never seen again.)[4]

Smallarms and flak took an even greater relative toll of marine and air force planes. This is partly because both those services flew a great deal more over South Vietnam and Laos, where the only enemy threat was gunfire most of the time. Even so, the figures are daunting: the air force lost 73 percent of its airborne casualties (87 percent of known causes) to guns, while the Leathernecks attributed 64 percent of all in-flight losses (and a whopping 97 percent of known causes) to gunfire.[5]

In numbers, these figures translated to roughly sixteen hundred fixed-wing aircraft shot down by smallarms or AAA from the total twenty-three hundred combat losses over Indochina. Admittedly, not all were jets. The navy toll represented OV-10s to F-4s; the air force losses ranged from little O-1 Bird Dogs to big, hulking F-105s. But let's not let anyone ever tell us again that guns can't knock down fast-movers.

OV-10

Gun positions were not invulnerable, however. Flak-suppression teams took a constant toll of AAA guns and undeniably reduced losses. Among *Essex*-class air wings, two- or four-plane detachments of F-8s were widely employed as flak suppressors. Later in the war, F-4s and A-7s usually filled that role from the big-deck carriers, but procedures were generally the same.

The suppressors flew on the flanks of a strike group, accelerating near the target to arrive fifteen to thirty seconds before the bombers. Spotting muzzle flashes on the ground, the pilots rolled in on the brightest flashes or those best positioned to threaten the strike birds.

Crusaders carried Zuni air-to-ground rockets in two packs, plus a full load of 20mm. The standard technique was a 45-degree dive long enough to get a good sight picture, then salvo the Zunis at about 4,500 feet. Pull the nose up about five miles, squeeze the trigger, and hose the flak site till the guns run dry. You were out of the run at 3,000 and into afterburner, rocketing back upward through the flak, which, if you'd done your job, wasn't quite as thick as when you rolled in.

Our intelligence folks told us we were inflicting tremendous casualties among enemy gunners and destroying or damaging large numbers of guns. Indication of accurate estimates came from two sources: a sharp drop in the NVA AAA order of battle in late 1967, coupled with our own reduced loss rate—well under three per thousand sorties.

But the fact remained the North Vietnamese never lacked for gunners, and the Soviets and Chinese kept them well supplied. If a guncrew was hosed by 20 mike-mike, punched by a Zuni, or spattered by a Snakeeye, it mattered little. Replacements were as close as the nearest rice paddy, and new guns were on the next freighter to drop anchor in Haiphong harbor. And access to Haiphong remained unimpeded until May of 1972.

Surface-to-air missiles appeared early in the North Vietnamese defense net, and remained for the ensuing eight years. Photorecon planes confirmed the presence of SA-2s southeast of Hanoi in April 1965, and the Soviets announced the fact to the world in May.

Despite this hard intelligence, no action was taken against SAM sites until several had been completed. We lost our first plane to the new threat on 24 July 1965 when an air force F-4C was bagged. The first strikes against SAM batteries came three days later—three months after the missiles were known to be available to the North Vietnamese.

Anti-SAM sorties were called Iron Hands, and numerous missions were flown against the new threat from July through August of 1965. But we were trying to play catch-up, and it cost us. The loss rate doubled in that short period. The SA-2s themselves scored several kills, but most losses were due to AAA fire. It was tough to fly in that mixed-threat environment.

A low approach to the target and low-altitude ordnance release kept us below the SAM envelope, as the SA-2 was at that time largely ineffective below 3,000 feet. But we hadn't counted on the effectiveness of pattern gunfire at low level, and this was where the prewar preparation for strikes against Cuba returned to haunt naval aviation.

The first successful Iron Hands were conducted in October 1965, but, even so, losses continued to mount. ("Success" was defined as *confirmed* destruction of a SAM site.) In late 1966 my squadron, VF-191, had twelve aircraft and eighteen pilots. In the first four months of combat we lost six planes—three to AAA, one to SAMs, and two in operational accidents. We received no replacement pilots for ten months, although new F-8s arrived. It was an embarrassment of riches, having more airplanes than pilots. In all, Air Wing 19 lost nearly half of its original seventy aircraft, destroyed or damaged.

It didn't have to be that way. We could have destroyed the SAM sites before they were completed, but the Johnson administration was fearful of offending the Soviets should some Russians have been killed in the process. General William W. Momyer, chief of the Seventh Air Force, recounted a discussion between General William Westmoreland of the army (in command of all U.S. forces in Vietnam) and Assistant Secretary of Defense J. T. McNaughton when McNaughton visited Westmoreland's headquarters in Saigon. "On a visit to Saigon at a time when my air commander, Joe Moore, and I were trying to get authority to bomb SA-2 sites under construction in North Vietnam, McNaughton ridiculed the need. 'You don't think the Vietnamese are going to use them!' he scoffed. 'Putting them in is just a political ploy by the Russians to appease Hanoi.'"[6]

Such was the gilded world view of the men who ran the war from Washington.

The Vietnamese were much more pragmatic. Originally they deployed their SAMs within thirty to forty miles of Hanoi. As more became available, they extended coverage along the northeast railroad to China, with lesser coverage for the northwest railroad. After 1967 there were usually two hundred active SAM sites in the country, with about thirty missile battalions in and near Hanoi. Eventually there was overlapping coverage of the Hanoi—Haiphong area, all the way south to Vinh.

Thirty SAM battalions equated to one hundred missiles on launchers, as a daily figure. Another one hundred SA-2s would be maintained at launch sites for reloads, with perhaps three hundred more in storage. In round numbers, five hundred SAMs were in-country at any one time. It wasn't a great many, but the resupply chain from Russia was uninterrupted for seven years.

A typical SA-2 battery consisted of four to six launchers deployed in a circle about fifty meters from a van containing radar and communications. Most sites had their own early-warning radar, code-named Spoon Rest, while the Fansong radar provided missile guidance. Batteries were linked by radio to central command posts, allowing volley or individual fire-control under a central authority.

By 1965 the SA-2 Guideline missile had been in service for at least eight years. It was a well-proven medium-range weapon propelled by a booster rocket that burned for about five seconds after launch. The sustainer took over following booster separation and provided another twenty or twenty-two seconds of burn, which translated into a slant range of twenty-five to thirty-one miles and a ceiling of nearly 60,000 feet.

The SA-2 warhead contained about 350 pounds of high-explosive that could be fused one of three ways: contact, proximity, or command detonation. If the mis-

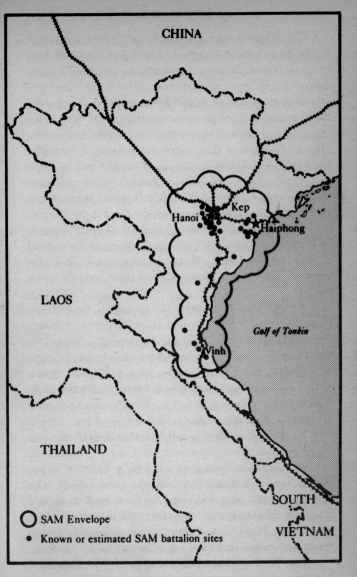

CHINA

Hanoi • Kep

Haiphong

LAOS

Gulf of Tonkin

Vinh

THAILAND

○ SAM Envelope
• Known or estimated SAM battalion sites

SOUTH
VIETNAM

SAM Sites and Coverage Early 1969

sile exploded within roughly three hundred feet of a tactical aircraft, it could cause lethal damage. Detonation inside two hundred feet almost certainly meant a kill.

Soviet doctrine called for missiles to be fired in pairs, with a few seconds separation. It was sound procedure. Most aviators had little difficulty evading the first missile if they saw it early enough, but while dodging that one they frequently failed to acquire its tagalong, which was the whole idea. And sometimes another one or two of the thirty-five-foot missiles were fired after a slightly longer delay.

Most SAMs arced down on their targets, providing better blast coverage from their warheads. Proximity fusing coupled with pulse control detonated the Guideline if radar information showed the intended victim opening the distance, since a jet making 450 knots passed through the SAM's lethal cone in under three seconds.

The key to beating SAMs was early sighting. For that reason, tacair pilots learned to avoid hugging cloud decks since the missiles could pop up undetected through the undercast. In reasonable weather, the telltale dust cloud, which indicated a launch, was the best visual cue. The dust cloud was quickly followed by a streaming white trail of burning nitric acid and kerosene—the second stage.

Timing was crucial in evading a SAM. If a pilot broke into his evasion too early, the missile had time to correct and continue tracking. If he waited a couple of seconds too long, he couldn't compensate in time. Surviving a SAM launch became an exercise in sweaty-palm patience and pulse-pounding judgment. Articulate aviators have spoken of the soul-searing experience of dueling with an inanimate object that pursued its prey with almost human intelligence.

But the missile was an aircraft, subject to the same physical laws governing manned aircraft. As the SA-2 approached detonation range, it small wings couldn't hack the Gs of a hard turn. Consequently, smart aviators always turned in two planes simultaneously to compound the difficulty of the missile's tracking. A barrel-roll turn, keeping the SAM 30 to 40 degrees off the nose, was optimum.

As the missile flashed past its intended victim, out of range, it usually went ballistic. Accelerating in a rocketing climb, the SAM would explode at 59,000 feet or thereabouts. Up in the thin air of the troposphere, the residue of the explosion lingered in an expanding black ring that radiated to huge proportions before finally dissipating.

One aspect of SAM combat benefited navy pilots with Cuban experience. It was known that any electronic beam guided to the center of a radar blip. With that knowledge, aviators found that they could fly the "SAM box," keeping closely enough together so that they would be painted as a single blip on an enemy radar screen and the missile would actually track between them. With the wingman in a two plane section seven hundred feet behind the leader in a 30-degree cone, stepped up or down, the SAM tracking to the center of the blip they constituted would pass just beyond lethal range of either aircraft. Only command detonation would set off the warhead, as the impact and proximity fusings were negated. Even then, the planes would still be beyond lethal blast range.

A seven-hundred-foot spread afforded most aviators ample room; they could jink and maneuver as a unit, remaining "in the box" almost indefinitely. But if they slid out toward a one-thousand-foot spread, they painted on a radarscope as two targets. One of them would be due for some unwelcome attention.

For all the hoopla accorded SAMs during the war, they inflicted relatively few losses. Fewer than two hundred planes were known shot down by SAMs from 1965 through 1972. Roughly 80 of them were navy planes, although proportionally carrier squadrons lost twice as many planes to SAMs as did the air force—15 percent of total losses vs. 7 percent. This statistical anomaly occurs because the blue-suiters flew only 43 percent of their sorties Up North compared with 52 percent of the navy's sorties. SAMs didn't appear outside North Vietnam until the spring of 1970 when SA-2s were reported in Laos. Even so, nearly one hundred twenty air force birds were knocked down by SAMs.[7]

Regardless of their relatively few kills, SAMs played a preeminent part in dictating the conduct of strike operations over the North. They were plentiful in Route Packs IV and VI. Aircraft inbound to worthwhile targets in those areas were often within the envelopes of thirty or more sites. By 1972 there were some three hundred SAM sites throughout the country, as far south as the DMZ, with some one hundred ten in and around Haiphong alone.[8]

The missiles complemented the guns exceedingly well. In taking evasive action to defeat the SAMs, aircraft inevitably were drawn to lower levels where gunfire became effective. And SAM evasion cost not only altitude but airspeed and energy as well. Having beaten the SA-2s, aircraft such as A-4s and A-6s were at a terrible disadvantage as they crawled back up to roll-in altitudes. Low and slow, they were vulnerable to new SAM launches or even to MiGs. A Skyhawk lugging a full load of bombs through 5,000 feet at something under 300 knots was not source of envy.

But help was on the way. In March 1966 the first Shrike antiradiation missiles arrived in WestPac. The new AGM-45s homed on radar beams, tracking them to their source and destroying the missile battery's radar-guidance van. At first the AGM-45As were limited to about two and a half nautical miles, but the B model increased effective range to around eight.

Shrike came as a decidedly unpleasant surprise to Oriental radar operators, and our intelligence officers began explaining that the folks Up North were having trouble getting people to sit in those funny little vans with revolving antennas on top.

When we went back into Route Pack VI in serious fashion, the loss rate was down where it had been before SAMs became troublesome. In fact, it was lower. Shrikes began interrupting Fansong and Firecan radars with disturbing regularity, and though the North Vietnamese adopted new measures to diminish the danger, they couldn't eliminate it. They never knew when a 390-pound missile would nest in one of their cozy little trailers.

Our own losses tell the tale. Through 1965, one

Grumman A-6 Intruder

out of seventeen SAMs would shoot down one of our airplanes. Beginning in 1966, however, twice as many SAMs would have to be fired to kill one of our aircraft. By the end of the war, the overall ratio—from start to finish—had risen to sixty SAMs fired per kill of U.S. aircraft.[9]

An Iron Hand section was composed of an attack aircraft—A-4 or A-7—packing two Shrikes, escorted by an F-4 or F-8 fighter. Within five minutes of the target, the fighters would break off as the attack craft continued on to their assigned SAM site. While the attack crews would focus on their scopes as the range to the target decreased, the escorting fighters would maintain a visual guard during the run-in. Usually the VA pilot lofted both Shrikes at the same target. What was good doctrine for the SAMs was good doctrine for the Shrikes. That left the fighters, if F-8s, to follow up the Shrikes in hope of finishing off the site. It wasn't hard to track the Shrikes, as they exploded in a brilliant burst of white phosphorus. Keeping the smoke in sight, a Crusader pilot normally cranked in 37 mils of elevation and fired out his 20mm load. At extreme range, four hundred-plus rounds would provide enough dispersion to saturate most missile sites.

Early in the war many SAM batteries were ringed with AAA. But because the flak sites themselves tended to give away the position of the SAM batteries, the Vietnamese opted for camouflage in favor of guns as the war progressed. Camouflage made more sense for two reasons: it cost less, and it made visual sighting by Iron Hand escorts and their cannon-equipped charges more difficult.

As one of the most experienced anti-SAM pilots— he flew more than fifty Iron Hands off *Oriskany* during 1967–68—Bob Arnold of VA-164 recalled, "Half our missile-firing detections came visually—the other half from our AGM-45 electronic listening. As the cruise went on we got smart and configured our A-4s with two Shrike and two Mark 82s on parent racks—no ejector racks. This gave us the mobility and flexibility to reattack a SAM site with bombs. On occasion our escorts would be an A-4 'slicked up'—just four Mark 82s, each one on a parent rack. This gave the maneuverability to stay with the Iron Hand bird.

"We had no practical way to train in the Iron Hand missions before we deployed in 1967, other than to listen to ECM tapes. Our OJT [on-the-job training] for new pilots who joined us during the deployment was to assign them the Iron Hand near Haiphong with a race-track pattern that flew over the water most of the time. That way, if they got bagged they would land in the water and probably be rescued."[10]

Another SAM-killer appeared in May 1968—the Standard ARM (Anti-Radiation Missile). The AGM-78 was bigger and longer-ranged than the Shrike and proved effective against both SAM and gun-laying radars. It wasn't always necessary to destroy the SAM sites or their radars in order to keep them from doing their job, however. "Passive" suppression—when simply the threat of Iron Hands (or the U.S. Air Force's "Wild Weasels") caused the enemy to refrain from launching, sometimes even from scanning—was often very effective.

But the opposition had the last word in the missile argument. SA-3s, with greater range and sophistication than the Guideline missiles, were operational Up North by early 1972, and that spring the man-portable SA-7 appeared.

First used in the Middle East in 1969, the Grail, as the SA-7 was known, was only five feet long and weighed only forty pounds. It was wholly passive owing to its infrared guidance, so airplane drivers had no way of telling when they were being tracked. The Grail operator merely followed his intended target through the optical sight of his shoulder-mounted launcher and waited for a green light. The green light told him that the missile was reading the IR signature of the aircraft, and he was ready to shoot. The effective range was greater than five miles. The Grail scored its first kill in Southeast Asia in April 1972.

Flying escort on Iron Hand sorties gave fighter pilots greater appreciation of the attack community. Perhaps the bravest man I ever knew, and one of the finest aviators, was Lieutenant Commander Mike Estocin of VA-192. We flew together in Air Wing 19 off the *Ticonderoga* in 1967, and Mike was on a roll. He seemed to wage a personal war against SAM batteries, and he wasn't content merely to suppress them. He wanted to destroy them.

On 20 April 1967 Mike led a three-plane flight against Haiphong, in the face of heavy SAM opposition. Mike called out the missiles, led his flight against three sites, and took out all three. But his A-4E sustained blast damage, and he pulled off to check his airplane. Satisfied he could stay in the air, he returned to the target to launch his last Shrike.

By the time Mike egressed, he was losing fuel at a horrible rate. He estimated that he had five minutes of flight time remaining. Providentially, a KA-3 tanker was close enough for him to plug in, and they flew formation back toward the task force. The Skyhawk was pumping fuel overboard through holes in the wings, as the KA-3 passed far more fuel than Mike was using.

None of us who saw that picture can ever forget it: the little A-4 hooked up to the "Whale," flying a long straight-in to *Tico* with Mike radioing instructions to the tanker pilot: "You're half a ball low, take it up." Mike Estocin was a precision aviator.

Finally, between two and three miles from the ramp, the tanker unhooked and pulled up. Mike was committed; he had fuel for one pass at the deck. Then his airplane caught fire.

But it didn't matter. He made an excellent landing, the fire crews doused the flames, and Mike opened the canopy. He tossed down his helmet to a crewman, alighted from the cockpit, and walked across the deck, not even looking back. Another day, another dollar.

Six days later I flew Mike's wing during a strike on petroleum facilities in Haiphong. It was the second Alpha of the day, with clear skies and unlimited visibility.

We coasted in ahead of the strike group at 21,000 feet, headed for Site 109 north of the city. As the strike pulled off-target and headed for the beach, Mike called, "The site is up!" We turned directly toward the SAM site.

Our radar controller, noting the strike was outbound, queried, "Are you feet wet yet?" Mike answered, "Negative," as we continued northward, my F-8 stepped up in a right-hand SAM box.

Moments later Red Crown came back: "The strike is all feet wet. What is your position? Are you feet wet?" There was apprehension in his voice.

I glanced over and saw Mike leaning forward, obviously looking for the SAM he knew would come. Then we both saw the liftoff, straight ahead about eight miles. Mike called it, and I acknowledged. The SA-2 arced up, the booster separated, and the missile continued head-on. I waited for Mike's turn to offset the SAM's heading, but we maintained course.

In retrospect, it's apparent what happened. Mike, the dedicated Iron Hand, was closing the range for a high-percentage shot at the site. He ignored the SAM, concentrating on firing a Shrike.

He waited too long. The SAM exploded off the

A-4's left nose, rolling the Skyhawk almost inverted to starboard. In a steep-diving, right-hand turn, Mike's airplane shed debris while trailing heavy flames from the belly.

Following, I was relieved to see the Skyhawk begin a pullout, coming level at about 2,000 feet. I was closing rapidly, and to prevent an overshoot I extended my speed brakes and finally had to lower my wheels and raise the variable-incidence wing. We were making about 160 knots, still decelerating.

Fire was visible from Mike's wingroot as I flew close aboard to starboard. I heard the high warble of another SAM closing in. My F-8 was rocked by the missile's passing and I felt the explosion behind me. It was that close. But I was more concerned with Mike.

Now very close to his right wing, I could see Mike leaning well forward in his seat, but he didn't turn to look at me. There was no response to my calls, so I went to guard frequency and summoned the ResCAP. We were directly over Haiphong, headed for the water, so there seemed a chance Mike could make it.

I crossed to port, and it was then I knew my hopes were baseless. The left nose and cockpit area were heavily damaged. The 350-pound SAM warhead had done its job. Mike's airplane had many large holes and the port intake was smashed. For lack of anything else to do, I crossed back to starboard. We were about three miles from the water, descending to 1,000 feet.

Then, ever so slowly, the Skyhawk began a left-hand roll. I followed to about 90 degrees, then realized Mike wasn't going to recover. I returned to level flight as the A-4 went inverted and seemed to hang in mid-air for a few seconds. Suddenly the centerline tank blew off and both Shrikes fired. The circuits apparently were burned through, punching off the drop tank and launching the missiles.

Then the nose came through and the Skyhawk impacted from inverted. I flew around the crash site at 500 feet, looking for a parachute.

There was none. Flak increased, and that was no place to be low and slow. The ResCAP, still inbound, asked if there was a chance. I said negative, and the CAP remained offshore as I came out.

Mike Estocin received a posthumous Medal of Honor and, more recently, a ship was named for him. His aggressiveness and airmanship were unquestioned. He got the job done, but he wanted more. We had kept the SAMs down while the strike went in and made a safe getaway. As soon as the bombers cleared the beach, our job was over.

Whether Mike chose to ignore the SAM launched at us or whether he misjudged its closure is open to conjecture. We did not turn even slightly so that the closure rate and proximity could be discerned better. Perhaps the SAM fooled him because it came from straight ahead.

In any case, Mike wasn't satisfied with merely suppressing the missiles. He wanted to shoot those people, just as he'd done six days before. But that was an inherent risk in playing the electronic game of tag over North Vietnam. The desire to win could overshadow one's sense of preservation, and it cost us some of our best men.

It's a lesson we will profit by studying.

5

THE AIRBORNE THREAT: MIGS

Find the enemy and shoot him down. All else is nonsense.

—*Baron Manfred von Richthofen*

Fighter pilots received much attention during the Vietnam War. And while the F-4 and F-8 jocks would never admit that the publicity lavished upon them was ill-directed, there is room for a sense of proportion. For in truth, the MiG threat was marginal. The North Vietnamese Air Force—including its Soviet, Chinese, and North Korean advisors—never came close to stopping U.S. Navy or Air Force strikes.

Not counting the bombing halt from 1968 through 1971, there were forty-four months of active or potential air-to-air combat Up North. In that time we lost seventy-six aircraft to MiGs, well under two per month. The persistent problem was not so much the number of planes we lost air-to-air, but the poor exchange ratio. Across the board, U.S. aviators eked out a 2.5 to 1 kill-loss ratio from 1965 to 1973. It was a mighty poor showing; in World War II and Korea, naval aviation alone claimed from between 8 and 14 to 1.

The 76 U.S. planes known lost to MiGs amounted

to less than 7 percent of all our fixed-wing aircraft losses Up North. Of the 473 naval aircraft downed over North Vietnam, 16 fell to enemy interceptors—only 3.3 percent. Even the air force's figures weren't extravagant (60 shootdowns by MiGs out of a total 618 losses Up North), although the proportion of air-to-air losses was three times the naval services', at 9.7 percent.[1]

Clearly, AAA and SAMs were the dominant threats to American fliers in North Vietnamese skies. But the losses inflicted by MiGs were more often than not unnecessary. We owned the air Up North; no navy strike was ever turned back, and probably very few air force formations were deterred from their targets by enemy action. But the MiG threat needn't have existed at all.

In August of 1964, the same month as the Tonkin Gulf incidents and air strikes against enemy PT-boat

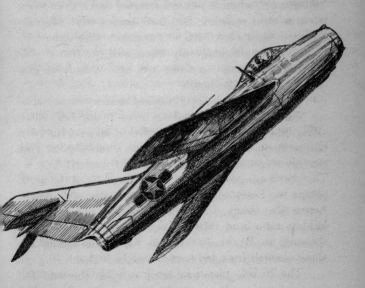

MiG-15

bases, thirty-six MiG-15s and -17s arrived at Phuc Yen airfield near Hanoi. Things remained relatively sedate in the air until April of 1965, when 17s jumped a formation of F-105s and gunned down two in the first conclusive engagement of the war.

By June the NVAF order of battle had doubled to seventy aircraft, and plans were afoot for the addition of supersonic MiG-21s. The latter were on hand by January 1966, by which time the North Vietnamese had established a thorough radar net in Route Packs V and VI. The radar net would eventually extend all the way down south.

Following Soviet air-defense doctrine, the NVAF established a tightly controlled fighter force almost totally reliant upon directions from ground-controlled intercept (GCI) stations. Their procedure was extremely detailed; controllers usually told pilots when to use afterburner, when to jettison external tanks, even when to arm their missiles. But their tactics were basically correct. Most early MiG engagements involved NVAF interceptors attacking only when well positioned with altitude advantage, making just one in-and-out pass before scooting for home.

Eventually some two hundred radars were installed in North Vietnam, linked to three major GCI sites: Phuc Yen, Kep, and Bac Mai airfields, all near Hanoi. A subordinate control station was later established at Vinh for interceptions in Route Packs I, II, and III.[2]

With complete enemy radar coverage of the aerial arena, we realized from the outset that we weren't going to sneak up on any MiGs. However, there wouldn't have been as many MiGs to worry about if we had gone after their main bases properly. Air strikes against the more southerly staging fields—Vinh and Thanh Hoa, for instance—were permitted fairly early in the war. But the airfields in Route Packs III and IV seldom had

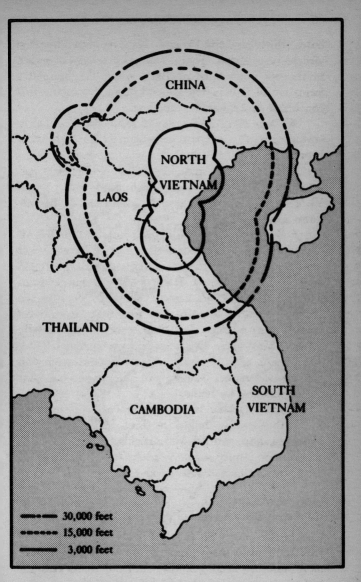

North Vietnamese Radar Coverage.

North Vietnamese Primary Air-Fields, 1972

full-time tenants. The home dromes around Hanoi such as Kep and Phuc Yen were where the MiGs lived, and those fields were immune until well into 1967, more than two years into Rolling Thunder.

The first strike against a northern airfield was at Kep in April 1967, prompting the NVAF to move many of its one hundred or so fighters to sanctuary in China. The first attacks on Phuc Yen and Bac Mai, plus Cat Bi near Haiphong, only came in October and November. At the time, these strikes were greeted with cheers from aircrews flying Up North, but the raids were intermittent. The on-again-off-again targeting reflected wavering policy in Washington. Consequently, the enemy's primary airdromes were only temporarily interdicted, with relatively few aircraft destroyed on the ground.

The fluctuating policy was evident to any aviator who read the newspapers that summer. Reports from the Middle East told of the Israelis' stunning victory over the combined Egyptian, Syrian, and Jordanian air forces in the first few hours of the June war. Some two hundred Arab planes were destroyed in their revetments while runway intersections were cratered in a thoroughly professional display of counterair operations.

So we had to live with the MiGs as an ever-present nuisance, and to counter the MiG threat, strike planning devoted much energy and allocation of assets to escort and combat air patrol (CAP). There were ForceCAPs over the task forces; BarCAPs as a barrier between the coast and our ships; MiGCAPs to prowl in Indian country; and TarCAPs in the target area. Such patrols were a constant drain on aircraft that could have been more profitably employed.

Any fighter jock worth his flight pay, however, relished the prospect of tangling with MiGs. Aerial combat was his stock-in-trade, was it not?

Well, that depended. When General Quarters

McDonnell F-4 Phantom

sounded in Southeast Asia, the navy fighter community was divided between not only two aircraft—the F-4 Phantom and F-8 Crusader—but two dissimilar missions. The mindset in each was drastically different.

The F-8 represented the tried-and-true approach to fighter aviation: a single-seat, single-engine dogfighter with gun armament augmented by heat-seeking missiles. The bigger, newer Phantom went the other route: a two-seat, twin-engine interceptor armed with radar-controlled missiles plus heat-seekers. But no gun.

The F-4's primary mission was fleet defense, which somehow became an end in itself. It was almost as if protecting the carrier was the aircraft's reason for being, rather than guarding the carrier from attack so it could launch strike aircraft. Consequently, the Phantom squadrons concentrated on long-range intercepts against inbound bombers. Radar identification and engagement with radar-guided Sparrow missiles was their goal in life. They were ill-prepared to tangle with nimble dogfighters eyeball-to-eyeball down in the weeds.

But the F-8 community had kept the faith. During the late 1950s and into the early 1960s, air combat maneuvering (ACM) was taught and practiced under enlightened leadership. The AirPac and AirLant commands allowed Crusader pilots to push the envelope, constantly improving their skills. Even when one of the young tigers finished an ACM hop dangling from his parachute, the higher-ups gritted their teeth and told the lads to get on with it. Grampa Pettibone, the bearded sage of *Naval Aviation News*, would exclaim "Sufferin' catfish!" or "Great horney toads!" and berate the offender in print, but it was understood this was part of the price one paid for proficiency in aerial combat. As the marines say, "He who sweats more in peace bleeds less in war."

Crusader pilots were rated by their peers on three points: gunnery, tactics, and carrier landings. Every F-8 squadron had its pecking order, and one's position in the unit had no relation to rank. If a hot young ensign put more holes in the banner or finished a hassle on a lieutenant's tail, he was regarded accordingly.

Gunnery became a fetish with F-8 pilots. Squadrons commonly spent three months or more each year at the ranges: Guantanamo Bay for AirLant squadrons, and El Centro or Yuma for West Coast units. They were gear-up with the sunrise, expended tons of ammo, and wore out hundreds of guns. The payoff came Up North years later.

Supersonic banner gunnery is probably the most difficult of air disciplines. Yet it accomplishes three important things: it keeps the systems and guns in good working order; it teaches the fundamentals of tactics; and it imparts great skill in maneuvering the aircraft to its limits. Anyone who can roll in from the perch at 42,000 feet, track a small target at supersonic speed while pulling six Gs at 30,000, and score hits, knows his business. He can fly the airplane smoothly and precisely, with his head out of the cockpit, where it belongs.

ACM was twofold: one-versus-one and "loose deuce" mutual support tactics. In man-against-man, each strove to reach his opponent's six o'clock position at 1,000 feet distance, optimum for a gun kill. When this occurred it was a clear victory, no questions asked. Room for argument arose when one fighter acquired angle-off the other's tail by minimum altitude. This was a win, but tainted.

Both positions, however, would permit good gun-tracking, and under combat conditions would allow a Sidewinder shot. After all, to reach a gunnery position a pilot has to fly through the AIM-9 (Air Intercept Missile) envelope.

The loose-deuce formation was a modification of the old Thach Weave of World War II. Patrolling in loose-deuce, two fighters were spread laterally between one and two miles, depending upon altitude. The abeam position was equal to the turn radius of both aircraft at that altitude and airspeed. Thus, loose-deuce allowed each pilot to visually clear a cone aft of his partner, outside the Soviets' Atoll missile range.

The wingman crossed from side to side during level flight to further clear the area. When the leader turned, the "wingie" moved in or out to maintain the abeam position.

Upon engagement the lead passed back and forth with a simple "I've got it," depending upon whoever had a visual on the bogie, or the better position. The other fighter usually went topside to provide cover and to position himself to better press the opponent should the attacker be unable to maintain advantage.

In this manner, one F-8 always remained on the stoop, ready to dive in and relieve its partner until the hostile was "had." Pressure on the opponent was therefore unrelenting, and regardless of how tightly he turned, eventually he would become vulnerable. No singe aircraft or pilot could survive a pair of expertly flown Crusaders.

In four-plane division formation, both element leaders flew loose-deuce while each wingman flew the SAM box, seven hundred feet astern in the cone and seven hundred feet up or down. When engaging, the formation split into two pairs and proceeded according to doctrine. When attacking more than one bandit, we took the most vulnerable and worked him as a single, keeping the others in sight and out of position. It was the ancient tactic of divide and conquer, applied to the third dimension.

The F-4 squadrons, being state-of-the-art in equipment and doctrine, seldom bothered with "outmoded" pastimes such as dogfighting. Besides, they had no guns and consequently felt little or no need to indulge in ACM. And the Phantom's early experience over Vietnam seemed to bear out the doctrine of long-range missile engagement. The first combat occurred south of Hainan as VF-96 engaged Chinese MiG-17s on 9 April 1965. The Sparrow launches resulted in a claim of one probable kill in exchange for an F-4B missing to unknown causes, perhaps fuel starvation.

Two months later VF-21 conducted a classic Sparrow shoot in which two *Midway* crews made a head-on intercept of NVAF fighters south of Hanoi. Uncle Ho lost two 17s in that brief set-to, and another AIM-7 kill went to VF-151 in October. However, only one more MiG fell to a Phantom between then and the spring of 1967. The communists began exploiting the maneuverability of their nimble little 17s, and suddenly the game changed. It was now a turn-and-burn, yank-and-bank contest, and F-8 drivers licked their chops, exclaiming, "This is where we come from!"

Hal Marr and company of *Hancock* bagged three MiG-17s in June 1966, and then Dick Bellinger of VF-162 dumped the navy's first MiG-21 in early October. The gunfighters had ridden into Dodge City and the opposition wisely cleared out of town. No other MiGs fell to navy pilots until the following April.

These early combats, while costing three F-8s, proved a great deal. We learned the necessary lessons and suffered no more Crusader losses in air combat for the rest of the war. But, equally important, the enemy was now known, cut down to size.

Going into the Tonkin Gulf shooting match, the MiG-17 appeared about six-feet-eight and the 21 seemed just about ten feet tall. It was widely accepted that two F-8s would have to double-team a 21, and in fact the loose-deuce formation was in large part based upon the fearsome MiG-21 threat. Squadron ready rooms had classified copies of the 21 pilot's handbook by the late 1950s, but the spooks who provided that dubious document did us no favor. The information was unreliable while perpetuating the myth of MiG-21 superiority. Crusader eventually scored four-zip against 21s.

It took a while to realize that the 21 was a point-defense aircraft, an interceptor. Unlike the 17, with its incredible turning radius, the 21 did poorly at low-to-medium airspeeds. It was an energy airplane all the way, relying on high speed and missile armament to get in, shoot, and scoot.

Flying four-plane formations like most of the world's fighter forces, the MiG-21s seemed to consider the first man as something akin to bait. The "leader" (if in fact he was such) headed a line-astern column with considerable space between MiGs. He might not get a shot, but he could stir up the Yankee formation, possibly presenting one of his trailing comrades with a quick setup for an Atoll attempt.

The Soviet Atoll was an imitation Sidewinder. The communists obtained at least two complete AIM-9s early in the 'winder's career and copied the design reasonably well. Since the Nationalist Chinese inaugurated the Sidewinder to combat over the Formosa Straits in 1958, the People's Republic MiGs were first on the receiving end. Reportedly a Nationalist F-86 pilot scored a direct hit during one of these hassles but the 'winder failed to explode, and the MiG driver motored home with a most unusual souvenir in his hide. A more pristine example allegedly crossed the West German border (eastbound) protruding from the rear window of a Volkswagen camper.

North American F-86 Sabre

Whatever the source, the Atoll was a reasonably effective heat-seeking missile. It was notably faster than the AIM-9B but considerably shorter-ranged, limited to an effective firing distance of about a mile and a half at typical combat altitudes. Atolls accounted for at least six of the naval air-to-air losses over Southeast Asia, with eight to guns and two unknown.

The navy's AIM-9D, widely used in the first half of the war, was a proven, reliable weapon. Simplicity was its main virtue. There weren't many wires or circuits to get scrambled during flight ops or from handling, unlike the more sophisticated radar missiles. But this isn't to say the Sidewinder lacked faults. Initially it sometimes failed to put away a MiG, because the warhead was only eight pounds. And AIM-9s were often in short supply. Incredible as it seems, *Essex*-class carriers almost never stocked enough 'winders in the magazines to fully arm all fighters embarked. Consequently, the same missiles were subjected to the rigors of hanging on the rails through catapult launches and arrested landings day in and day out. Add to this the stress of manhandling by beefy ordnancemen, and the AIM-9's success rate becomes remarkable.

Originally the Sidewinder "went stupid" for eight-tenths of a second after launch, during its enabling period. Then it began to track the heat source of its target, assuming the infrared signature remained within the gimbal limit of the seeker head (that is, the arc through which the seeker was allowed to move). Later models tracked from the rail right through launch, allowing the "smarter" AIM-9s to cut the corner on a maneuvering target and actually rendezvous with it instead of overhauling from astern.

The Sparrow was another story. Although Sparrow was the F-4's primary weapon, it simply did not perform well. It wasn't reliable in combat, despite optimistic assessment from the Pacific Fleet Missile Range in peacetime. Even when it might have worked, the rules of engagement often militated against its use. Visual identification of bogies was a cornerstone of fighter ROE, but the Sparrow was intended to shoot down radar blips—not close-in, maneuvering fighters.

After the war a study of fighter weapons concluded the AIM-7 suffered from at least four flaws. Pilots had a tendency to ripple-fire, which did bad things to the Sparrow's efficiency rating. Instead of shooting one missile or two, they'd unload all four.

Switchology also was a factor. Launching a Sparrow involved a fairly complex procedure of radar tracking and locking-on, coordinating between the pilot and back-seater, and setting the switches in the correct sequence. The system was fine for engaging distant bombers, but rather cumbersome in a dogfight.

Another factor was the Sparrow envelope, on two points. Like the Sidewinder, the AIM-7 had maximum and minimum parameters for a successful shot, but the Sparrow's minimum range was much greater than that of the AIM-9. That, coupled with difficulty in visually recognizing the inner and outer edged of the envelope, was another complication. Firing parameters change with altitude, airspeed and temperature—a combination guaranteed to spoil one's concentration in combat.

The fourth flaw was the reliability of the missile itself. Its complexity meant that extreme stresses were imposed upon the Sparrow's innards during the ordinary course of a working day, especially on a carrier. Under such rough circumstances, sophistication proved little advantage.

The bottom-line readout is as follows: The percentage of Sidewinder attempts and successes was almost an identical flip-flop of the Sparrow's. Lumping in all missile firings by all three services, AIM-9s scored 58 percent of the missile kills in 40 percent of the launches. Conversely, Sparrows accounted for just 38 percent of the kills in 54 percent of all missile attempts. The missing factor is the Air Force's AIM-4 Falcon with merely five kills. Thus, the radar birds—Sparrow and Falcon—gained only one kill in eleven or twelve attempts. The simpler heat-seeking AIM-9 was successful every 5.5 firings.

Gunnery placed second in overall kill probability with 7.5 attempts per confirmed kill. Gunfire was third in outright numbers with forty-seven MiGs. Therefore, 20mm guns disposed of nearly as many MiGs as did Sparrows (fifty-two), though the Sidewinder remained the champion killer with a tally of eighty. The lesson is clear: simple weapons work best.

While playing with numbers, it's instructive to briefly consider the kills per engagement of F-4s and F-8s. Crusaders logged twenty-five MiG engagements from 1966 through 1968 in scenarios ranging from one-versus-one to four-versus-many. They rang up eighteen kills for an efficiency rating of 0.72. In other words, when an F-8 jock went into a fight, he had nearly a three-in-four chance of winning his Silver Star.

Between 1965 and 1968, navy F-4s recorded merely twelve MiGs downed in thirty-nine combats, or 0.30 kills per engagement. During 1972, however, the Phantoms ran hogwild, bagging twenty-four MiGs in twenty-three combats for an "impossible" rating of 1.04 kills per engagement. The reason: vastly improved training in the F-4 community during the slow-down phase of the war from late 1968 through 1971. During that time the Phantom folds opened the Naval Fighter Weapons School, of which more later.[3]

From the start to finish the navy F-4s knocked down thirty-seven MiGs in sixty-two combats—a rating of 0.59 kills per engagement. Air Force Phantoms had

0.14 kills per hassle, and their exchange rate looked better in comparison. Naval Phantoms finished at 5.42 kills per loss while the blue-suiters' F-4s ended at barely three to one.

By virtue of F-8 success early on, and a tremendous sprint by navy F-4s toward the end, naval squadrons recorded a box score of 3.5 kills per loss, including all aircraft types. The air force ended at 2.28 to one.[4] How to explain the difference?

The difference, in a word, was training.

The Crusader clan, as previously noted, was wholeheartedly devoted to ACM. Mission-oriented at the grass roots and supported by enlightened leadership from the head offices at AirLant and AirPac, the F-8 squadrons lived and dreamed fighter combat. They were allowed to risk airplanes while perfecting their skills—a factor largely overlooked today. The knowledge gained through trial and error translated into confidence and ability when the shooting started.

The press-on attitude was further enhanced by a thoroughly professional, surprisingly critical spirit of give-and-take, regardless of rank. In the better squadrons the debriefs resembled perhaps the self-criticism of a communist cell meeting. Comrade X might criticize himself for going low instead of high against Comrade Y, even if X were senior to Y. As long as the comments stayed in the ready room, they were accepted and absorbed. But woe betide Lieutenant (jg) Y if he were so gauche as to remind Lieutenant Commander X of the event while patronizing the O Club that evening.

When the whistle blew in late '68, signaling halftime in the Southeast Asian War Games, the navy stood back and took a hard look at the scoreboard. Over half the points put on the board by navy fighters had been posted by the "second-string" F-8s. They were older, less sophisticated, less capable than the F-4s in the starting lineup. Clearly, something was wrong. The Crusader's six-to-one kill-loss ratio proved it. No other aircraft approached the F-8 success rate.

During the next year naval aviation took two critical moves. It began transitioning F-8 instructors to F-4s as a means of imparting ACM knowledge, and it founded the Fighter Weapons School, a.k.a. Topgun.

The nickname was ironic. Navy Phantoms never did have guns, contrary to the air force, but the message was clear. Topgun, founded as an adjunct to VF-121 at Miramar, convened its first class in March 1969. Its charter had been written by Captain Frank Ault, commissioned to study the reasons for the overall poor showing by F-4 squadrons in aerial combat. His conclusions stressed the need for specific ACM and weapons training, with establishment of a pool of hardcore specialists to go forth and preach the gospel of air combat.

To its lasting credit the navy—not always known for abrupt reversals of policy—admitted that Ault's criticisms had merit. Topgun quickly gained independent status as a separate command and formulated doctrine largely based upon existing knowledge. Applying sound principles of maneuver and weapons employment, the Miramar postgraduate course turned out a new crop of MiG-killers. Where the F-4 squadrons had been trading two MiGs per Phantom in 1965–68, they bounced back in '72 with a startling twenty-four-to-two score: an exchange rate of twelve-to-one.

This dramatic reversal proved two truths. Training was everything: "You fight like you train," said ace Randy Cunningham, and it became Topgun's motto. But also worth noting was a less-cited dictum: quality aviators are more important than gadget-loaded airplanes. The pilot is not merely half the equation in fighter combat. He is in fact more than the sum of his aircraft and its systems. We Americans have a tendency to trust technology more than skill, but we periodically rediscover the truth.

The F-4's tremendous success in 1972 was conclusive proof of the importance of man over machine. ACM doctrine and training, evolved from the F-8/Topgun talent pool, turned an interceptor armed with radar missiles into a lethal platform capable of maneuvering into favorable firing position for heat-seekers. Only one of the navy's twenty-four kills from January 1972 to January 1973 was scored with a Sparrow.

Another aspect of the pre-1968/post-1971 naval air war helps illustrate the dramatic difference equally well. But it has somehow not gotten the attention it deserves. We refer to the losses of navy attack, recon, and tanker aircraft to enemy fighters.

The first such casualty occurred in 1966 when ChiCom MiG-17s shot down a KA-3 that had strayed over the Hoihow area of southern China. Three other losses occurred in 1967: an A-4C in April and two A-6As off *Constellation* in August. Finally, two *Coral Sea* A-1s

Douglas A-1 Skyraider

were jumped near Hainan in February 1968, and one was shot down. Thus, of five VA losses to enemy aircraft before the bombing halt, four were knocked down by Chinese fighters. Only the A-4 fell to a NVAF MiG.

In absolute numbers, these five planes amounted to extremely small losses. It may even be claimed that they prove how little effect the MiGs had upon the air offensive Up North. But two things rankled: they needn't have been lost at all, and they were destroyed largely with impunity by the Chinese.

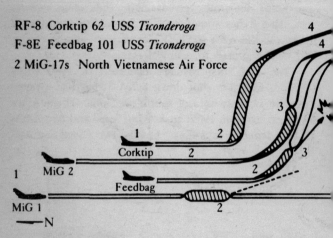

RF-8 Corktip 62 USS *Ticonderoga*
F-8E Feedbag 101 USS *Ticonderoga*
2 MiG-17s North Vietnamese Air Force

1. Starting positions.
2. Lead MiG sighted; Corktip breaks port. Second MiG shoots at Feedbag, misses.
3. Feedbag fires AIM-9, misses. Second MiG disengages.
4. Lead MiG turns between two F-8s.
5. Feedbag hits with second AIM-9; MiG slows.
6. Feedbag hits with guns; MiG crashes.
7. F-8s reform and search for MiG wingman.
8. F-8s egress toward coast.

MiG Engagement, 9 July 1968

In 1972–73 the situation was much improved. An RA-5C became the only navy plane lost while under escort by carrier fighters since 1967. Thus, Vietnamese fighters shot down exactly *two* navy strike-recon birds during the entire war. That statistic speaks well for the protection afforded by Phantoms and Crusaders.

The escort record was compiled under circumstances both complex and adverse. Because of the enemy's good radar coverage over his homeland, we expected to begin every engagement at a disadvantage.

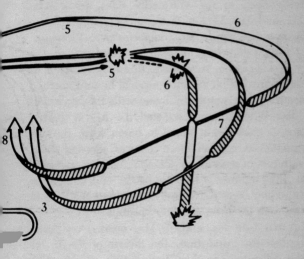

------ Gunfire

———▸ AIM-9 shot

⟫◁▭▭▭◁ Bellyside

The MiGs could launch, remain low until in position, then pop up with little or no warning. Only an excellent lookout would keep us from being fatally surprised.

A normal Alpha strike had only four TarCAP fighters between the bombers and the threat axis. In the face of a more accomplished enemy air force, we might have found ourselves short of fighters, even by calling the MiGCAP and BarCAP fighters. The Iron Hand (anti-SAM) escorts could be detached in a pinch, but that would have left single A-4s or A-7s alone and vulnerable deep in the unfriendly skies. As it was, MiGCAP and TarCAP flights accounted for more than two-thirds of the navy's aerial victories over Vietnam.

Giving credit where it seldom existed before, the subject of A-4s in an ACM mode deserves mention. A case can be made that an unintentional benefit accrued to Crusader pilots simply by flying with the Skyhawks every day. When Topgun selected the A-4 as a MiG simulator, it chose well. Small to begin with, the A-4 had a smokeless engine; these features afforded thousands of hours of practice in detecting bandits. In aerial combat, first sighting is half the battle, and more than one MiG-killer owes much to flying around the boat in company with his little "Scooter" friends.

Not that A-4s were entirely MiG meat. They broke even against the opposition. Ted Swartz of VA-76, for example, unloaded a pod of Zunis into a 17 almost in Kep's traffic pattern. And we should recall that two of the navy's first ten MiG kills were scored by pro-driven A-1H Skyraiders. The moral is obvious: a good driver in a clunker can beat a Gomer Pyle in a hotrod.

But even experienced aviators can make mistakes, and in fighter combat the winner is generally the pilot who capitalized upon his opponent's errors. That's what happened during a photo recce from the *Ticonderoga* on the afternoon of 9 July 1968. The RF-8 pilot was

Lieutenant William Kocar of VFP-63, flying Corktip 602. I was a lieutenant commander in VF-191, flying the CO's F-8E, Feedbag 101.

Kocar had about ten targets to photograph, and we were on the west side of the Song Ca River, southbound towards Vinh. The surprising thing that day was how much AAA we drew everywhere we went. It seemed as if the North Vietnamese were prepared for us, as indeed events proved.

We were about twenty miles inland, and, given the gunfire, I thought the RF-8 was a little too low for comfort—only about 2,000 feet above ground. Consequently, I was stepped up higher than usual, maybe as much as 3,000 feet, in a right-hand loose-deuce. Our airspeed was good, between 475 and 500 knots.

Looking back toward seven o'clock, I saw a green MiG-17 about two miles behind Kocar, closing very fast. The overtake was probably 150 knots or more, and there wasn't a lot of time to act. I shouted, "You got a MiG behind you, Corktip!"

I quickly followed with a repeat, "We have a MiG out here," to the shipboard controller. Well to the south, orbiting in another F-8, was *Tico*'s air wing commander, Phil Craven. A former squadron CO and long-time friend, Phil never carried any strain. His deep voice penetrated the chatter: "All right, settle down. Come on up with your call sign."

"This is Feedbag One. Stand by, I'll get him!"

While all this conversation went on, Kocar pulled a fantastic hard port turn, causing the speeding MiG to overshoot badly. I had already started a hard nose-low turn as tracer sparkled past my right wing. So there were two bandits. I ignored the wingman to gain position on the leader.

I got a good Sidewinder growl with about five Gs on the airplane and a look-down of about 30 degrees.

Those extra feet of insurance altitude were now evident as a mistake; I was just a shade too high to get a really good angle on the MiG.

The AIM-9 tried hard. It guided toward the 17 and almost made the turn. Flying outside the MiG's tilted starboard wingtip, the 'winder exploded but inflicted no visible damage.

Then the MiG driver made a fundamental—and fatal—error. He reversed his turn from port to starboard, lighting his afterburner as he rolled wings-level. I fell directly in trail at one mile, one G, and fired my second Sidewinder. It was a direct hit, I believe, right up the tailpipe. The sky suddenly filled with what looked like small pieces of metal but the MiG was still flying in one piece.

However, the 17 was decelerating very fast and I was closing quickly. I popped the speed brakes to avoid an overshoot and, in the limited time available, acquired a decent sight picture. With the pipper on top of the MiG I fired 167 rounds, scoring about six to ten hits. The airplane was raked from fore to aft across the top and came apart. I passed close aboard, cleaning up the F-8 and accelerating to start looking for the MiG's friend. Later we learned that when the wingman saw his leader go down, he called it a day.

Kocar saw the 17 fall and exclaimed, "Way to go, Feedbag!" Thirty-five seconds had passed.

I was pumped up, working on an adrenaline high. It took Phil Craven to bring me back in the cockpit with a calm, "Come on, let's settle down a little bit." Kocar and I briefly discussed prospects of photographing the wreckage but we decided to head out. We rejoined, cleared one another's six, and headed for the tanker. Phil drawled, "Think you can get the airplane aboard now, John?"

My voice was now down within three octaves of normal: "Goddam, CAG, I'll sure try."[5]

That little set-to wasn't won over the Song Ca river. It had been won in 2,800 hours spent from Norfolk to Jax to Gitmo and Miramar. It was won in hundreds of passes at towed banners in 30,000-foot gunnery runs, developing a feel for the airplane and an eye for weapons use.

Later an intelligence officer showed up with a typed page worth of data on the late lamented MiG driver. He had about 450 hours total flight time, including 250 in-type. Not a great deal, but it should have been enough to hack the program with his initial advantage. The Vietnamese had set up the situation pretty well. Apparently they had analyzed the pattern of our photorecon flights and capitalized upon our predictability. They staged the two 17s down to Vinh, where the section launched and then trailed us to a favorable point before beginning their fast run-in to gun range.

But the MiG leader probably never saw my Crusader. He acted as if he were concentrating solely on the RF-8. Otherwise he'd never have sandwiched himself between two hostile aircraft. Or perhaps he counted on his number two to handle the escort. If so, the trust was misplaced. His wingie left him in deep serious and split. That was one debrief we Crusader jocks would have liked to hear.

Debriefs, however, were a big part of a later exercise involving four F-8 pilots and the air force F-4 wing at Udorn, Thailand. In August 1972 the chief of staff in *Hancock* summoned me. "We have a request for F-8 pilots to fly with the Air Force and teach them tactics. Just be tactful." And away we went.

I had two pilots from VF-211 and another from VF-24. On arrival at Udorn I was driven to a general's office and he said, in effect, "We used to know this stuff, but we forgot it. We haven't taught it in years. We believed those days were over. I'm afraid we didn't keep the faith." He was right. The air force kill-loss ratio in 1972 was even lower than it had been up to 1968. Some five hundred MiG engagements by USAF fighters in the last eighteen months of air combat generated only seventy kills. And in June 1972, the air force actually came up short: two kills for seven losses to MiGs. They managed to break even in July at six-all.

Frankly, they were terrible. In VF-124 or 174 (the F-8 training squadrons on each coast) the *students* completing a basic tactics course could whip anybody I flew with at Udorn. The air force tactics were entirely predictable and standardized. The pilots were still flying the World War II finger-four as a basic formation. All that accomplished was to set up the outside trailing planes—numbers two and four—as heat shields for the lead and number three.

The F-4s were "Sparrow-tuned." They seldom maneuvered in the vertical plane, even with all the power in the F-4. In combat they did everything at the same place and same speed, about 450 knots. They kicked off their external tanks by slowing at the same spot every time. And guess where the MiGs were waiting.

I began by sitting quietly as the blue-suiters briefed and debriefed. But we could see this wasn't going to work. I had to become an instructor again, and the situation was somewhat strained. But I knew the air force jocks were under pressure from on high, so I stopped acting like a guest. I began conducting briefs and, more important, debriefs. Our hosts became our students; it could not be otherwise.

There were a lot of tight jaws, but slowly the Udorn folks began to come around. It was a matter of showing them the path of righteousness to ACM. It took some doing, though, for the unbelievers had strayed far from the fold. In the end, it was like getting a vegetarian to eat steak. You give him a taste.

The contest between their F-4s and our F-8s was so uneven that at first we were almost ashamed of the disparity. I tried to keep my three pilots from becoming intolerably cocky and overbearing—especially at the O Club. We did our best to accomplish what we'd been sent to do. But it was too late in the game to effect any significant results. When we left in September, the war was to last only four more months. Although one of the Udorn squadrons was the top MiG-killing outfit in the air force, it was the exception since the 555th reportedly specialized in air-to-air combat.

The sight that remains in my mind from this experience is a chilling one, for any number of MiG pilots must have seen identical views: the pitiful spectacle of four super aircraft in front of you, all tucked in close finger-four, pulling a level turn. An Atoll fired anywhere in parameters would find itself in the position of the proverbial mosquito in the nudist colony. It would hardly know where to begin.

In summary, it is my strong belief that, by keeping the faith, the F-8 community was largely responsible for both the navy and air force establishing their excellent fighter weapons schools. The Crusader clan showed that ACM was here to stay and that it could be mastered. But service memories are short. I only hope that in a few years, when a planner looks at an area to cut— especially high-accident flying—he won't be allowed to reduce ACM practice. Yet the indications are already there. The air force is leaning more toward hanging bombs on its beautiful little F-16s, and at least one vice admiral (a former F-8 pilot to boot) has said that what were previously national assets have become national treasures and must be treated accordingly.[6]

Which raises the question of fighter aircraft design philosophy. The KISS principle (Keep It Simple, Stupid!) has been abandoned, and with increasing complexity has come increased cost. A drastic rethinking is needed, and soon. It should be obvious that if a government cannot afford to lose a combat aircraft, it cannot afford to own it. For if the airplane is owned, it must be flown to justify the expense. And if it is flown, especially in ACM practice or for real, it stands a good chance of becoming a $30 million hole in the ground.

Yet consider the false economy. Preserving high-price fighters by prohibiting realistic, practical training will surely lead to even greater losses in combat. If the squadron-level lessons of Vietnam taught us nothing else, they proved that very point; negatively with the F-4 and positively with the F-8.

We were fortunate over North Vietnam. The opposition air force never seriously hurt us, never prevented us from bombing any permitted target. But we lost airplanes and aircrews unnecessarily, and we had to come from a long way behind to catch up. Next time we cannot count on having time to play catch-up.

And next time is one day closer with every sunrise. Check six. And keep the faith.

6

ECM: THE ELECTRON WAR

*He who wins by deception deserves no less credit
than he who wins by force.*

—Nicolo Machiavelli

Electronic warfare had matured during the late
1960s. Events in Southeast Asia and the Middle East
proved that modern air combat required electronic
countermeasures (ECM) and even counter-countermeas-
ures (ECCM) for both offense and defense.

Electronic warfare (EW) came of age in World War
II, when it was used primarily in antisubmarine and
night-fighter operations in the Atlantic-European theater. Germany and the Allies exchanged the technological lead throughout the war. Both the German U-boat
campaign and the British night-bombing offensive
depended in large part upon the electronic advantage.
Advances in centimetric radar and in detecting or jamming sensors and communications set a precedent for
the future.

The unique wrinkle over North Vietnam was the
surface-to-air missile. Because SAMs dictated strike
warfare tactics, defeating or confusing missile scanning
and guidance became paramount. Not only equipment,

but technique and doctrine constantly evolved on both sides.

The U.S. Navy entered the war with one aircraft devoted to ECM. The propeller-driver Douglas EA-1 Skyraider had seen combat in Korea, when AD-5Ws and -5Qs represented the top of the line. Following the 1962 designation change, they became the EA-1E and -1F, respectively.

Another Douglas product, the big twin-jet Skywarrior, also served in the ECM role from 1968. But the vintage "Spads"—prop-driven Skyraiders—remained carrier aviation's premier EW aircraft for quite some time.

The "Electric Spads" (EA-1Fs) flew with a pilot, a commissioned aircrewman known as a naval flight officer or NFO, and two enlisted men as ECM operators. The airframes and avionics were 1950s construction, featuring vacuum-tube technology and manual operation. By mid-1965 the fleet contained twenty-one EA-1Fs and "Fat Spad" -1E models on the East Coast with VAW-33, and seven AirPac birds in VAW-13. Greater need in the Tonkin Gulf, however, resulted in the West Coast detachments taking twenty EA-1s by 1967.[1]

Even so, this was a very small number of platforms for so valuable a mission. Consequently, VAW-13 operated a forward-based unit at Cubi Point in the Philippines. Each "det" consisted of two planes and crews, with ten to twelve maintenance personnel. Ideally, a combat-experienced pilot was teamed with a "nugget" NFO, or vice-versa.

The ECM crews lived a gypsy life in WestPac. They rotated up and back from Cubi—eight hundred miles from Yankee Station—on thirty-day tours, regardless of changes in carriers. It wasn't unusual for a VAW-13 detachment to fly from six carriers in six months.

Standard "armament" for the EA-1F consisted of two sensors, two jammers, and often two chaff dispensers. Full 20mm loads were carried, but they were seldom used as there were plenty of "straight" A-1s to work ResCAPs and fly strikes. Although the ECM gear was antiquated by 1960s standards, it was effective when employed by skilled, experienced aircrewmen. Thorough knowledge and a delicate, almost artistic, touch were necessary to make the equipment work well.

Under any but ideal circumstances, optimum jamming range was twenty to twenty-five miles, though nearly twice that distance was possible. Consequently, ECM coverage of strikes was usually conducted three to four miles offshore after 1965. A *Midway* EA-1F was clobbered by AAA in April of that year, and the valuable ECM birds were kept out of harm's way as much as possible thereafter.

As a result, the Electric Spads concentrated on covering ingress and egress points for the strike groups. During Alpha operations, two to four EA-1s were airborne constantly, with individual crews double- or triple-cycling to cover multiple strikes. Thus, while an F-4 or A-6 was usually back aboard ninety minutes after launch, the Skyraiders often logged three to five hours per sortie, sometimes more.

Because the jammers were directional, EA-1s had to fly directly toward or away from the enemy radar for best results. Usually fifteen to twenty miles out, the Skyraider pilot began a slow inbound descent at 110 knots. Recalls one pilot: "I liked to start at 8,000 to 10,000 feet and descend to 4,000 or 5,000 as I got closer to the site, often with gear and flaps down. Then I'd apply climb power, pulling up gear and flaps, and let the torque roll the aircraft inverted. I'd split-S, which put me on a reciprocal, with optimum jamming. This little maneuver also could help screw up any possible sharp-shooting SAM operator."[2]

With the standard two EW aircraft airborne, and

each carrying two jammers, up to four radars could be neutralized simultaneously. The electronic spectrum was usually represented, from the lower S band to the highest X band. In-between was the L band, generally employed in gunlaying radar. But the Spads carried passive receivers for each band, which showed "grass" across the bottom of the screen.

When a radar site came up for a look, the ECM operator saw a line peak on his scope, which indicated the enemy frequency. The airman then turned to a second scope with the telltale source dot in the center of a compass rose. A lobe about the dot showed the relative bearing, with the radiating transmitter's location known by the center of the lobe. Although there was no range indication on the scope, experienced operators could often provide accurate estimates based on image and signal strength.

Having identified an active radar, the ECM operator returned to his first scope. The magnetrons in external pods were tunable across an arc, but they worked best straight-on, hence the direct descent at 500 feet per minute toward the site. The electronic warrior manually tuned his jammer to superimpose the image over the spike on his screen. When the jammers were activated, they turned the opposition's radar scope to snow.

The North Vietnamese soon learned to tune their spikes up and down the band, seeking enough clear time to allow a firing solution for guns or missiles. But adept operators could match the enemy's tuning efforts, keeping the jammer on the laterally moving spike. It became a cat-and-mouse game, involving not only skill but guile. Each player tried to anticipate his opponent's likely moves, with the advantage favoring the jammer. He didn't have to completely overpower the enemy transmitter; all he had to do was disrupt operations long enough for the bombers to get in and out.

If the jamming aircraft were singled out for unwelcome attention, the ECM crew played with the radar for as long as prudence allowed. The descent inbound was timed to arrive at about 2,500 feet when the operator could no longer "break the lock." The aircraft then was vulnerable to a SAM launch.

Against more powerful land-based transmitters, the airborne sets were unable to compete at closer ranges— say four to six miles, if they got that close at all. Consequently, the EA-1 pilot told his crewmen to let him know when they could no longer break the radar lock. At that point the pilot retracted his wheels and flaps, applied full power, and torque-rolled to the left in a split-S. This maneuver lost about 1,500 feet, taking the Skyraider below the briefed 2,500-foot minimum effective range of the SA-2. Recovering on a reciprocal heading, the Spad pilot added power, climbing into a chandelle to perhaps 5,000 feet heading outbound. Airspeed seldom exceeded 110 knots, which afforded adequate control of the aircraft. The evolution was repeated as often as necessary. Then the jamming aircraft orbited well offshore until the next strike went in.

One VAW-13 flier shook up his former squadronmates in the fall of 1967. Detached to Eglin Air Force Base, Florida, the NFO observed tests of SA-2s captured by the Israelis during the June war. He was astonished to learn that minimum effective altitude was closer to 1,500 feet, and he hastily posted a letter to that effect. This revelation, coming via unofficial routing, was received with some chagrin. But the "zappers" adjusted their safe altitudes and continued providing ECM support in the Tonkin Gulf.

Another means of blinding radars was metallic chaff: aluminum strips cut to various lengths corres—ponding to know radar frequencies. Chaff originated early in World War II and was called "window" by the RAF. It had limitations. When the airplane dropped chaff, the frequency band was clogged with false targets, but because the chaff could not move forward with the plane, its protection was short-lived. The dispensing aircraft, and those flying through the area, quickly outpaced the area where the strips drifted to earth.

In naval warfare, chaff was intended for uses other than covering strike groups. Chaff could shield ships from electronic detection, for example. Fleet exercises showed that cruising disposition for a typical task force could be covered by three layers of aircraft: chaff-dispensing EA-1s at 10,000 feet; EF-10 Skyknights at 15,000; and EA-3s or air force EB-66s at 20,000. The Douglas aircraft were capable of obscuring ships from electronic locations as long as the chaff remained airborne, which was a considerable period because of its light weight.

The Skywarrior first appeared in an ECM role in 1958 with delivery of the A3D-2Qs. Twenty-five were built, crewed by seven men including four EW operators. These big birds were redesignated EA-3Bs in 1962 and in 1968 were joined by thirty-nine multipurpose EKA-3Bs. These latter electronic-tanker variants were seldom regarded as satisfactory. Tanking was the "Whale's" main contribution to the Tonkin Gulf Yacht Club, and the addition of ECM packages to the tankers only denigrated the plane's primary role.

Furthermore, there were too few A-3s is it was. They were the largest airplanes operated from carriers, and most *Essex*-class ships, for example, embarked only two. Few in number and with an important mission, A-3s weren't risked over the beach. Only one was lost to enemy action in the North Vietnam arena, when it strayed over the Chinese border and was shot down by MiGs.

The EA-3s were operated by VAW-13 detachments,

as stopgaps while we awaited the new generation EW aircraft. The navy had let a contract in 1966 for what became the EA-6B, Grumman's ECM version of the Intruder. Some twenty-seven EA-6As, modified from conventional Intruders, were produced for the Marine Corps, and thy retained some strike potential. The EA-6B, however, was essentially a different airplane—devoted solely to electronic warfare.

While paving the way for the Prowler, the EKA-3s served two purposes: they tested new avionics and electronics; and they afforded ECM operators combat experience. But the Litton equipment installed in EKA-3 testbeds reportedly gave serious trouble early in the program, and Electric Spads had to fill in the gaps aboard some ships.[3]

Maintenance crews seized upon this situation to indulge in some merriment. Aboard the *Coral Sea*, somebody went to work with a stencil. It wasn't long before deckhands and aircrew began noticing a neatly stenciled, official-looking logo on some of the Zappers' Skyraiders, in anticipation of more Electric Whales. Under the horizontal stabilizer, right where the navy paint specs called for such things, was "Simulated EKA-3." Another said, "On loan from the Smithsonian Institution."

When the EA-6B entered squadron service in January 1971, it was evaluated by VAQ-132 at NAS Whidbey Island, Washington. The Scorpions already had experience with EKA-3Bs in the *Coral Sea, Ranger, Enterprise,* and *America*. One-Thirty-Two made the Prowler's first combat cruise with Air Wing 8 in *America,* arriving in the Tonkin Gulf in July 1972. This was only six months before U.S. air operations ended over North Vietnam, but it was enough to show the Prowler's promise.

EA-6Bs carried a four-man crew: a pilot and three NFOs. The right-front seat was occupied by an officer responsible for navigation, communications, defensive ECM, and chaff. The rear two seats were for ECM operators, each covering half the electronic spectrum.

The Prowler was a quantum leap in electronic warfare. Its advanced sensors and jammers, most of which were automated, allowed greater standoff capability. Hard-core Skyraider operators, however, insisted they could do just as well with their vacuum-tube equipment and manual tuning before EA-1s disappeared from Yankee Station in 1968. But there was no denying the EA-6B offered options previously unavailable. With automatic tuning, multichannel/multisite capability and omnidirectional equipment, the ECM war escalated to new levels.

And the twin-jet Prowler could haul a bigger load. Some EA-1F pilots recall being told that they were not to jettison their ECM pods in event of engine trouble. The avionics were more valuable than the airplane, so there was no point bringing back the Spad minus its underwing stores! The EA-6B suffered a fearsome loss rate to operational causes, something which cannot be said of the Skyraider. Apparently there was nothing wrong with the Prowler itself. But it was generally flown by pilots with relatively little experience, and the airplane was usually bigger and heavier than anything they'd flown previously.

Regardless of the ECM platform—Skyraider, Skywarrior, or Prowler—the effect was much the same. Successful jamming forced SAM batteries to fire ballistically, without benefit of radar guidance. Jamming could also interfere with the North Vietnamese fighter-direction network, a bonus. Communist air doctrine called for ground-controlled intercepts, and if the controller was unable to talk to his pilots, the system broke down.

With regard to their fighter-direction network, the opposition could be cagey. Often when we identified a fighter-direction channel, the North Vietnamese played tape-recordings on that frequency while actually directing over another.

All tactical aircraft operating over the North were supposed to have their own electronic countermeasures, or at least warning of tracking. Beginning in the summer of 1966, most navy aircraft had the ALQ-51, aimed at the Fansong B radar. Chaff and infrared dispensers were seldom available before 1969. Even then, there were never enough black boxes or dispensers for training. Precombat information often consisted of little more than listening to tapes of the electronic warbles that indicated enemy radar scanning and tracking. The shortage of ECM gear was critical. A carrier leaving Yankee Station occasionally had to pass its black boxes to the relieving ship so the new air wing would have enough to go round.

Through it all, the name of the game was information. Constant surveillance was conducted by electronic intelligence-gathering (Elint) aircraft: big EC-121 Constellations from Thailand, EB-66s from South Vietnam, and Task Force 77's E-1s and E-2s in the Gulf. Elint activities picked up in early 1968 and remained at high levels thereafter.

By the end of 1969 the opposition's Fansong radar had been modified for earlier arming of SAMs, which in turn allowed a lower engagement altitude. This occurred during the four-year hiatus in Rolling Thunder. During that time only reconnaissance sorties were flown over the North, though the much-publicized "protective reaction" strikes occurred throughout 1971. While the bombing had ended Up North, such forays at least permitted aviators to keep an eye on electronic warfare developments and make adjustments as necessary.

Grumman E-2 Hawkeye

The navy's strike and fighter aircraft underwent a complete metamorphosis in the ECM realm during the war. For at least the first three years the large majority of carrier planes flying over the beach were electronically naked. This was caused by the navy procurement policy, which emphasized obtaining "platforms" in preference to systems. It may have made economic sense in peacetime, but in wartime it was false economy. The opposition matured rapidly Up North, and Task Force 77 aircrews frequently were vulnerable to enemy radar scanning and tracking.

To deal with his unacceptable situation, naval aviation robbed Atlantic Peter to pay Pacific Paul. East Coast squadrons were nearly stripped of radars and ECM black boxes to supply the air wings deploying to the Tonkin Gulf, It was a risky move. The Sixth Fleet in the Mediterranean, within reach of Europe, Africa, and the Middle East, has traditionally been of greatest strategic importance since World War II; there would have been hell to pay if even a moderate threat had arisen in that arena.

The electronic deficit was finally made good. By

1969 or thereabouts the decision makers had recognized ECM procurement as critical, and measures were taken. With black boxes such as the ALQ-94, tactical aviators could defeat SAM fusing and even knew on their radarscopes the direction of the threat. This, in addition to the heart-pounding audio warning of a low-warble/high-warble tone which distinguished scanning radar from tracking, provided adequate warning. Knowing when a SAM was aimed at your aircraft made a big difference, and frequently we could break the missile's lock with chaff dispensers.

As we entered the last year of aerial activity over North Vietnam, new gadgets appeared on both sides. SA-3s were reported active in January 1972, and the chief of the Soviet Air Force visited Hanoi in March. Apparently the Russians indoctrinated their acolytes in new techniques during this period, for multiple SA-2 engagements were reported thereafter, featuring track-on-jam and optical tracking. They also adopted high-low engagement tactics in an attempt to trap evading aircraft that dived to lower levels.

Two episodes from Air Wing 9 will illustrate the increased threat level from SAMs, as well as improved jamming capabilities. Both episodes occurred on 10 May 1972 and concerned pilots from the *Constellation* who had shot down MiGs earlier in the day.

Lieutenant Randy Cunningham and Lieutenant (jg) Bill Driscoll of VF-96 had killed three MiG-17s in a frantic hassle near Haiphong. They disengaged, joined by another Falcon F-4J, and headed outbound, climbing through 22,000 feet. At that point Randy heard an urgent call, "SAM, SAM, SAM! Nam Dinh!"[4]

There was no electronic indication of a launch, and the F-4s ECM gear had worked as advertised so far. But Randy glanced to starboard and, sure enough, a SAM was closing rapidly on his airplane.

Beginning a break into the missile, Randy saw the SAM explode. He felt the concussion, banked to port, and rolled out. His instruments showed normal, and he accelerated northeastward. Then the Phantom pitched into a nose-high roll. Randy got it under control, noticing he'd lost his primary hydraulic system. By then the backup system was losing pressure, and the utility gauge was fluctuating. The stricken F-4 rolled again, and Randy lost all doubt as to the seriousness of his situation. The only control he maintained was with power and rudder.

Alternately using afterburner to bring his nose up and rudder to roll the nose down, Randy kept the burning fighter headed for the water. He briefly spoke with Driscoll, confirming that they would stay with the airplane as long as possible. Bailout over that area of the North meant certain capture.

At the mouth of the Red River, the Phantom exploded, its tail blowing off and the rest of the plane dropping into a violent flat spin. The pilot and radar operator ejected, landing just offshore and within range of smallarms. They drew sporadic gunfire, but, providentially, two marine helicopters from the USS Okinawa arrived to rescue them.

At the time it was assumed Cunningham and Driscoll's ECM gear had failed. With knowledge acquired since then, it is more likely the missile that tagged their F-4J was guided electro-optically. Only that one was fired, contrary to usual practice, and that piece of information further supports the optically guided theory.

Late that same afternoon VF-92 launched an F-4J as escort to an A-7E Iron Hand. The Phantom pilot was Lieutenant Curt Dose, who had begun the day's MiG slaying when he dropped a 21 almost in Kep's traffic pattern. Curt had mounted an 8mm movie camera on his instrument panel, but he was too busy to turn it on during his supersonic chase through the weeds. This time, however, he had the camera running as he entered the target area.

Haze, limiting visibility, prevented early detection of the SAM launches. Curt glimpsed a missile emerging from the murk and wracked his aircraft into an evasive turn—then he saw two more in close trail headed directly for him. He knew SAMs were command- as well as proximity-fused and these were too close too fast. There was no time even to eject. He was resigned to dying at that instant.

But he didn't. Nothing happened. All three missiles continued their ballistic path to oblivion. Later, two frames of movie film showed the SAMs close aboard, passing narrowly in front of the F-4.

When he got back aboard the *Connie*, Curt Dose looked up the EA-3B detachment. He was told the Prowlers had monitored twenty SAMs in the air at that moment—too many to jam all tracking or guidance frequencies. So the alert ECM operators quickly switched their efforts to the detonation frequencies, with total success.

Curt paid off his debt in true fighter-pilot tradition. He gave the electronic warriors a full case of Jack Daniels.[5]

The last word in electronic warfare came from the opposition, less than five months before the cessation of air operations Up North. In mid-September a large SAM knocked down an F-4 despite all efforts to defeat it. Code-named "Fat Black," it was a new kid on the SAM block and it seemed immune to jamming. Although it took out the Phantom, the marine crew ejected safely and was rescued.

In the years since Vietnam, EW aircraft have further increased in importance. Today, because of their effectiveness, ECM birds would be priority targets in a shooting war. As Ernie Pyle said of aircraft carriers in World War II, it's a precarious honor, but a proud one.

7

STRIKE WARFARE, CV STYLE

The airplane lends dignity to what would otherwise be a vulgar brawl.

—*Anonymous*

Power projection is what carrier aviation is all about. The pundits have all manner of phrases and buzzwords to describe the exercise, but what all the effort amounts to is placing violence in the opposition's back yard.

The advantages of the aircraft carrier were convincingly demonstrated in Korea and Vietnam. In both wars, shipboard aviation projected power ashore against a continental mainland. In World War II, in contrast, power was projected against isolated islands. When dark-blue Corsairs, Panthers, and Skyraiders appeared over the Pusan Pocket in 1950, that was power projection at work—and it proved the importance of territorial independence. If we had had to rely on landbased aircraft in Japan, we would have found that we lacked the ability to provide quick-response tactical airpower because of range and endurance problems. When gray-painted Phantoms, Skyhawks, or Intruders cycled from the Tonkin Gulf to South Vietnam and over Laos and

Up North, that was mobility. Because we owned the sea, we owned the sky.

Carrier air off Vietnam operated in two basic forms. Cyclic operations under Rolling Thunder were sustained, bone-wearying evolutions usually conducted for three days at a time, twelve hours per day. Alpha strikes were more in line with World War II doctrine: three per day with perhaps an hour between each recovery and launch for a total of six to seven hours. It was still hard work, often more dangerous than Rolling Thunders, but easier on all hands and more satisfying.

The difference between the two types of operation was the level at which the targeting was determined. Alphas, because they took place in Route Packs V and VI, were almost exclusively the province of Washington, be it DOD or the White House. Orders would trickle down the chain of command to CTF-77 and the CarDiv commanders. Rolling Thunders generally originated with the task force. Knowing the approved targets and operating areas, the admirals commanding the airpower afloat largely ran their own shows.

Once the operation reached Yankee Station level, both cyclic and Alpha operations proceeded along similar lines. Targeting, for example, was based largely upon photoreconnaissance, though other sources of information were also considered. If the spooks believed a target existed in an area, although the birds hadn't flushed it, it often made sense to dispense with recce flights. They might tip off the opposition. Better to announce one's intentions with the roll-in of the lead bomber.

The carrier division staffs assigned targets, and the various ships' operations offices passed on the orders to air wing commanders. CAGs* and their intelligence

---

*In 1963 the navy's carrier air group (CVG) organization was redesignated carrier air wing (CVW) for similarity with air force terminology. Previously a CVG was led by commander of air group—CAG, for short. Despite the air wing designation change, CAG remains in common use even today.

folks went to work planning ingress and egress routes, plotting troublesome defenses, and assigning specific targets. A practiced intel-admin staff could lay out an operational plan in a couple of hours.

Briefing for all pilots, aircrew, and spares generally began ninety minutes before launch. In the first half-hour, the briefers discussed the overall picture, providing an intelligence summary and assigning sectors for armed reconnaisance and, should the recons fail to turn up anything, designating end targets. Also covered were weather, enemy order of battle, and recent tactical trends. If new AAA or SAM batteries had appeared, they were noted. Whenever MiG threats increased or changed in any way, they were described as well.

These threats were always, of course, of much interest. Standard procedures evolved for dealing with them, as Rolling Thunders usually followed similar patterns. In the words of one A-4 pilot, "Two-plane road recces in North Vietnam would encounter AAA on some targets of opportunity. It would track us or lay in wait until we pulled off. The rule was no multiple runs on a target, or if you did go back you would vary your roll-in point and duration of run—always jinking coming off the target."[1]

Communications, an important topic, was viewed with ambivalence. A good air wing seldom needed radios inbound to the beach. The old pros could launch, form up, hit the tankers if necessary, and go feet dry without a transmission. So comm briefings were often terse notations of strike and search-rescue frequencies. CAG might offer a few comments about radio discipline, such as, "If you're hit, get off strike freq." What he meant was, "Shut up and die like a man."

Such an attitude was not actually as callous as it seemed. If a damaged plane were still flying, it could probably make the coast, in which case there was nothing for the others to do but press on. But if somebody had to punch out, ResCAP would be there as long as any chance for a rescue remained. The important point was to keep the strike group intact.

Following first briefing in the intelligence spaces, pilots and aircrew returned to their ready rooms for more detailed planning. Tactical considerations such as order of run-in, approach and roll-in headings, and so forth were all determined. So too were the sequence of detachment for Iron Hands and flak suppressors. Ordnance fusing and ECM procedures were among the other topics discussed.

Emergency procedures and SAR "safe areas" were reviewed, including designations for preferred bail-out points and the locations and call signs of rescue helos. Each flier also reviewed his personal ID information—the three questions and responses that would help confirm his identity to a chopper crew attempting a rescue.

After that, it was time to head topside and man up. Toting their helmet bags, aviators, laced into their G-suits and loaded down with torso harness, assorted survival gear, and lucky charms, trudged up to the flight deck. Some extremely competent aviators frequently stroked rabbits' feet or palmed silver dollars while walking to their planes. Despite college degrees and extensive technical knowledge, some men preferred the extra advantage perhaps conferred by a favored amulet.

It was considered good form to conduct a quick walk-around inspection of one's aircraft. Most fliers did so in a purely perfunctory manner, knowing plane captains and deck crews had already inspected each plane. Others, a decided minority, scrutinized all control surfaces, safety wires, and ordnance pins.

A delightful bit of whimsy appeared in *The Hook* in 1984, under the nom de plume of Lieutenant Butch Blaster. Entitled "Real Aviators Don't Eat Quiche," the article provided the definitive how-to last word on manly conduct around navy aircraft. The author advocated dispensing with such formalities as preflight inspections, noting "that's what mechanics are for." Real Aviators were advised, however, "to make a great show of checking the side number before manning."[2]

In the real world, one hard-charging F-8 pilot was renowned for his casual attitude towards walk-arounds. He was a genuine kick-the-tires-and-light-the-fire type of aviator, brought to account by students and mechs at Cecil Field. When the gung-ho pilot jumped in the cockpit and tried to start, he discovered the boys on the ramp had towed an engineless Crusader to the parking area.

With the ship steaming into the wind for an Alpha, launch proceeded as briefed. Ordnance pins were pulled, ejection seats armed, canopies locked, and wings extended. Pilots followed directions of plane handlers as the catapult crews placed each aircraft in position. Engines were brought to maximum power and pilots and launch officers exchanged ritual salutes. Then the exhilarating rush as the steam-powered cats flung airplanes off the deck. Whether it was an A-4 grossing 20,000 pounds with fuel and ordnance biting into the air or a huge KA-3 tanker weighing 73,000 pounds lifting off, the procedure never failed to fascinate me: from zero to 160 knots in three seconds.

Within fifteen minutes after the four standby fighters were catapulted to replace the BarCAP, the strike group had assembled over the ship. The attack planes usually launched when the duty BarCAP was halfway home to the task force. In that time the sections and divisions had reached their assigned altitudes and were orbiting five miles from the ship. Then, usually under radio silence, the formation fell in with the CAG and proceeded on course, climbing to about 22,000 feet.

Strike composition for an Alpha varied little throughout the war. A maximum effort from an *Essex*-class air wing typically involved twenty bombers—sixteen A-4s and four F-8s—with two A-4 Iron Hands and their Crusader escorts on either side of the strike birds. A two- or four-plane TarCAP took station on the side most likely to encounter MiGs, while four F-8 flak suppressors flew opposite. A MiGCAP section or division brought up the rear.

In addition, an EA-1 or EA-3 remained offshore to provide electronic support. A pair of KA-3s, and frequently a section of A-4s with "buddy packs," also stood by to provide airborne fuel. And two helos awaited at the northern SAR station. One chopper would launch as the strike set out; the other would wait as back-up.

In all, an Alpha consisted of about twenty-eight to thirty-two planes with the strike group, plus five to seven other aircraft in supporting roles over the Gulf. Big-deck air wings employed very similar tactical formations but with different aircraft. F-4s filled the fighter role. The A-6s and A-7s (following transition from Skyhawks) brought the number of bombers close to thirty.

As the Alpha strike approached the coast at 20,000 to 22,000 feet, the leader keyed his mike and voiced a terse "feet dry" to the radio watch some fifty miles offshore. By now pilots would have flipped the switches in their cockpits that armed the guns, bombs, and rockets. The ordnance was "hot."

So was enemy radar. The long-range height-finders like Firecan arced through their azimuths, registering in aircrews' earphones as rhythmic bleeps. No danger yet; the opposition was merely sizing us up, pulling in information. Soon heavy-caliber gunfire would begin and continue sporadically along the route.

To counter the barrage fire and to initiate approach to the target, the strike leader would begin a slow

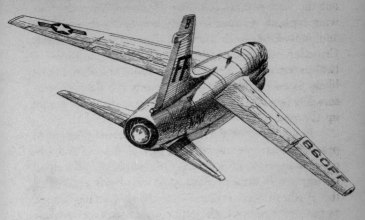

Vought A-7 Corsair

descent from his coast-in altitude. This procedure also allowed the aircraft to begin accelerating, building the momentum necessary to counter SAMs and reduce exposure to AAA. The angle of descent was determined by proximity of the target to the shore—whatever descent rate was necessary to arrive over the roll-in point at 12,000 to 14,000 felt above ground level.

During those 8,000 to 12,000 feet of descent, the F-8 bombers had their work cut out. The Skyhawks, lugging a full bombload, seldom made more than 350 knots, and the sleeker, more powerful Crusaders were hard-pressed to remain with the formation. Yet they had to keep station if the attack was to be coordinated. They had one of two choices: weave far to the sides at decent airspeed to avoid running away from the A-4s; or get nose-high and slow, hoping they had enough energy to dodge a SAM. Phantoms flying with A-6s and A-7s had similar problems.

Inevitably SAMs would come up during the approach. There was no way to take out all the possible

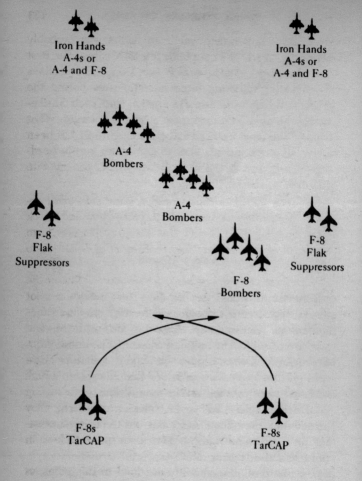

Iron Hands
A-4s or
A-4 and F-8

Iron Hands
A-4s or
A-4 and F-8

A-4
Bombers

A-4
Bombers

F-8
Flak
Suppressors

F-8
Flak
Suppressors

F-8
Bombers

F-8s
TarCAP

F-8s
TarCAP

Plus 2 or 4 F-8s deployed along threat axis on MiGCAP

Plus 1 or 2 EA-1s for ECM and 1 or 2 KA-3 tankers, all offshore

Representative *Essex*-Class Alpha Strike, 1967

sites, since any target worth an Alpha was probably within the reach of a couple dozen SAM sites. The best bet, therefore, was to detach the Iron Hand sections shortly after initiating letdown. The sites posing the greatest threat were usually known, and each Shrike-armed bomber was assigned a priority target. That would have been handled in briefing: "Site 91 has been active all week and sits almost astride our run-in heading. Pirate, you take that one. Maverick, you hit Site 104 over to the northeast."

The A-4/F-8 sections would require no verbal order to detach themselves from the formation and attack their targets. They knew the setup well enough to break off at the proper time, accelerating ahead or to either side at the right moment.

Despite our suppression, SAMs were a fact of life Up North. It would not be long now before a pilot would hear over his earphones the high-pitched tones of Fansong, warning him of an approaching SAM. The guidance frequencies were subject to jamming from ECM birds offshore, but the SAM operators were cagey. They knew they couldn't come "up" for a look without exposing themselves to a Shrike or revealing their frequencies. So, while tracking regularly, they turned on their guidance channels for the briefest possible period; the odds were good for a quick lock-on in the few seconds' exposure.

Radio discipline should have held to this point, as most pilots were alert to electronic warning. But once the SA-2s began to fly, no-rad went out the window. The key to beating SAMs was seeing them early, and as soon as aircrews spotted them, warnings and instructions flew back and forth over the airwaves: "Two SAMs, two o'clock low. Break right! Break right!"

Now came the risky part of ingress. The risk lay not so much in being hit by a missile but rather in losing altitude and airspeed in the course of evasion. The hard, descending turns that best defeated a SAM robbed pilots of height and energy, sucking them ever more deeply into the shooting gallery of AAA and smallarms that abounded in Route Pack VI.

Sometimes, in the frantic maneuvering to out-turn a SAM, wingmen or element leaders lost touch with section or division leaders. Then it was a long, lonesome climb back to altitude, hoping to rejoin the strike group before the attack began. An *Oriskany* Skyhawk pilot, Bob Arnold, describes just this situation from 1968:

"I led an Alpha strike to a target six miles outside Hanoi. We approached at 12,000 feet, plus or minus 500, with no AAA or SAMs until two minutes from our time over target. From that point we had thirty missiles and every goddamned gun that could fire. A couple of planes got shot up, all of us were forced down. Only two of us—my wingman and myself—made it to the target. He missed and I laid a string of eight or ten Mark-82s on target. We exited the area at 500-plus knots (no centerline tank) at 50 feet or less, violently S-turning all the way because my ECM gear told me a SAM was tracking me. It turned out to be overly sensitive equipment, but at the time we only knew that the damn things were deadly."[3]

Under such conditions, pilots were most vulnerable to being jumped by MiGs, but the MiGCAP and TarCAP fighters considerably diminished this threat. The bread-and-butter job for F-4s and F-8s was "trolling for MiGs," and the pilots had been briefed on the most likely axis of approach from nearby airfields.

The NVAF knew how to dangle a MiG as an enticing bit of live bait for eager fighter jocks. A call from "Red Crown," the fighter-direction ship in gulf, wasn't an open invitation to go hunting. "Blue Bandits airborne at Bullseye" meant 21s launching out of Phuc

Yen; it did not necessarily mean, "Go get 'em tiger."

Most air wings rightly cautioned the MiGCAP against chasing bogies forty to sixty miles away. The fighters' job was to protect the strike birds, and they did superbly well. The loss of only six bombers or support aircraft to MiGs through the entire war speaks volumes for navy fighter doctrine and air discipline.

Besides depleting fighter cover for a strike, the North Vietnamese, by dangling MiG bait, hoped to lure unsuspecting pilots over AAA or SAM batteries. A zealous fighter pilot could be sucked into a flak trap by a juicy decoy. After a while a pattern emerged: the NVAF drivers often feinted toward navy formations but shunned combat. They would only engage when numbers or position (or both) seemed to favor them.

As the formation neared the target, the aircraft would be down around 15,000 feet. The flak suppressors accelerated ahead, timing themselves to arrive from thirty seconds to two minutes before the strike birds. From 10,000 to 12,000 feet the suppressors spotted the largest muzzle flashes on the ground, quickly decided which guns were high-threat, and rolled in.

Ideally, the wing tanks would be empty by now. You're more likely to take a hit in the wings than in the fuselage because of the wings' greater surface area. For obvious reasons no pilot wants a hit in a fuel tank.

A high-angle dive on AAA batteries gave an unsurpassed view of the objective. As the suppressors dropped down, they lined up the gun sites in their illuminated reticles, trying for the optimum picture. Then, from about 4,500 feet, they released their Zunis or Rockeyes. F-8s hammered away with their 20mms. Abrupt, high-G pullouts had the suppressors out of their recoveries by about 3,000 feet above the ground, pulling off target just as the first bombers dived in from their wagonwheel orbits.

Each strike pilot's dive heading had been assigned

at briefing. Properly executed, the attack came from
three or more directions. This had the effect of splitting
the defenses. An interval of about ten seconds allowed
each pilot a view of the target sufficient to position his
pipper for an accurate drop. In 45- to 60-degree dives
the bombers—sporty little Skyhawks, F-8-lookalike Corsairs, or bulbous-nosed Intruders—slanted down through
5,000 feet. Like the flak suppressors, they held the
drop to about 4,500, bottoming out no lower than 2,800
above ground level (AGL).

Then it was nose-up. Crusaders and Phantoms lit
the after-burners and rocketed upward at 60 degrees or

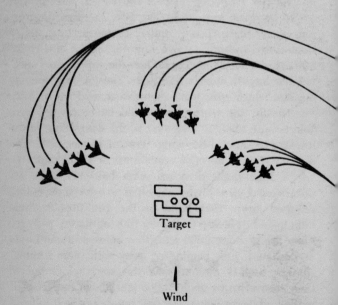

Typical "Wagon Wheel" Attack Pattern

better. Height was life insurance coming off-target. It got a pilot out of smallarms and light-caliber flak quickly and gave him room to maneuver against SAMs. If worse came to worst, height afforded invaluable time to nurse a damaged aircraft to the water or toward a "safe area" for ejection.

Doctrine called for egress by sections. Element leaders and wingmen reformed, pursuing an irregular, high-speed course eastward to the coast. True, a straight line was the shortest distance to the beach, but it was also the most predictable. Course changes of up to 60 degrees, coupled with frequent altitude variations, made

Roll-in point 12,000–14,000 feet above ground level.

120° bank, 45° nose-down.

Drop at 4,500 feet, 450 knots.

4- to 5-G pullout. Top out at 18,000–20,000 feet. Egress by sections.

Aircraft intervals of 10 to 20 seconds, a few degrees variance in bombing heading.

Entire strike on and off target in under 2 minutes.

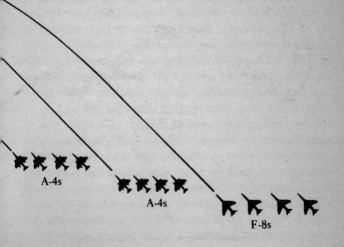

it difficult for enemy gunners to work out their fire-control solutions and also provided the pilot with an all-around view of the possible threats.

By the time the last planes had left the target area, about three minutes—and one or two eternities—had elapsed. The mental and physical energy expended in concentrating on so many things in so short a time was immense. Altitudes, headings, switchology, sight picture, recovery altitude, threat awareness—all these factors had to be put together in an equation whose hoped-for result was survival. Each detail demanded intense attention, and each in turn was replaced in one's consciousness as priorities changed at 400-plus knots.

Eventually the beach passed below and behind. "Feet wet" was the radio call. Each aircraft checked its partner closely, looking for visible damage, leaking fuel, hung ordnance. If all appeared normal it was a routine matter of hitting the tanker or making directly for Marshal—the entry to the landing pattern—and land aboard.

Routine: how easily humans fall into that frame of mind. Is a mid-air refueling "routine"? You have to slow up to the tanker's speed with a minute amount of visible overtake, finesse the controls with almost imperceptible movements to plug the receptacle into the weaving basket, and advance the throttle home. Following contact, the fuel line always undulates. Suck in the previous JP fuel, unplug, then head for the boat.

Is landing a jet aircraft aboard a pitching, rolling ship "routine"? You cock the aircraft's nose up, play with the few knots of airspeed that science and gravity have granted, and keep the illuminated ball even with the horizontal datum lines on the deck mirror. Adjust rate of descent with power and crunch onto the deck within 160 feet or so from the stern to snag one of the arresting wires. Routine.

Returning sections or divisions were about 1,000 feet apart, compressing the traffic pattern to the limit. As one plane rolled wings-level on final, the angled deck was still probably occupied by the plane that had just trapped. It took practice, a keen eye, and well-developed judgment for the landing signal officer holding the waveoff switch to determine whether the plane on deck would taxi clear in time for the approaching pilot to get aboard on this pass. All the while the LSO's talker would maintain a running patter describing deck status: "Foul deck. . . . Foul deck. . . . Foul deck, gear set, Skyhawk. Foul deck. . . . Clear deck!" Seconds later another A-4 would hook onto one of the wires.

A debrief always followed, providing a summary of events and results. But few strikes were documented in anything like the style of World War II actions reports. Not even the MiG engagements were assembled in written form until Project Red Baron (analysis of air combat over North Vietnam) began in 1972. By then, of course, the war was almost over. When the Red Baron reports were completed and finally analyzed years later, it was far too late to apply the data.

So went the cycle, two or three times a day for Alphas. It became routine. Brief, launch, fly the mission, return, debrief. On Rolling Thunders, the cycle times were even more intense and went on day after day. A typical Rolling-Thunder line period went something like this.

The *Essex*-class carriers launched about eighteen planes per cycle while the next mission briefed. About fifteen minutes were consumed in launching the birds spotted on deck, and then recovery of the airborne mission began almost immediately. The effect was akin to a busy railway station, with arrivals and departures occurring constantly.

The unheralded folks in this unceasing evolution

were the plane handlers and directors. They would direct the recovered aircraft to the forward elevator and give an abrupt crossed-arm "halt" signal. The plane would be lowered to the hangar deck, where it would be taxied aft, spun about, and inspected. Rearming and refueling would begin almost immediately, and the "gang on the roof" continued launching aircraft.

The procedure continued for about twelve hours, typically from 0400 to 1600 or from 1300 to 0100. Unlike Alpha strikes, which were flown only in daylight, Rolling Thunder sorties proceeded regardless of darkness. And even as missions were being organized, launched, and recovered, the air boss would still have to work in other carrier aviation chores. Tankers had to be launched, BarCAPs relieved, helos cycled in and out. Management skills were at a premium.

So were energy and endurance. It wasn't unusual to find a dirty, grimy plane handler curled up in a handy corner, sound asleep, sometimes still wearing the "Mickey Mouse" ear protectors and plastic goggles. Coming off duty after several noisy, windy, dangerous hours, the youngsters handling planes, servicing cats, or loading ordnance often slumped wherever they could find a spot.

The tractor drivers were super—they had to be. Eighteen- or nineteen-year-olds you'd think twice about trusting with your car in a hotel parking lot wheeled multimillion dollar machinery around the cramped space of a flight deck. Working their tractors and towbars largely on their own, these teenagers fitted aircraft into positions frequently only a few inches larger than the planes' wingspan. If two F-8 pilots parked side by side wanted to test their folded-wing droop flaps, they'd have to take turns. If they tried it simultaneously, the flaps would collide.

Preflight checking of aircraft often proved difficult.

Aircraft were packed so tightly together that it would sometimes be impossible to go between them; many times the rear one-third of a fuselage was completely inaccessible—it was dangling over the water. Flight-deck turnarounds were another interesting endeavor, especially in a bird like the Crusader where the pilot sat six feet ahead of the nosewheel. Following the director's wands on a dark night, pivoting around the nose gear, the pilot could only trust that the young man with the wands knew where the deck edge was. For during half the arc of that pivot the nose of the aircraft was well over the water, in total darkness.

Night landings, of course, were always sporty but the sportiest of all were those performed under radio guidance when visibility was down near zero. A carrier-controlled approach (CCA) is almost identical to a ground-controlled approach (GCA), with the difference that the runway is moving at twenty knots or more, probably pitching, rolling, and/or yawning. Nevertheless, CCAs were commonly flown with sixty-second intervals. In one-minute gaps, aircraft broke out of the Marshal pattern—flown in left-hand turns with vertical stacking—and began to follow a line downwind from the ship. Speed control was the key; the pilot would alternately accelerate then decelerate and pop then retract speed brakes, flaps, even gear. The goal was to reach the departure point from Marshal behind the previous pilot at the sixtieth tick of the second hand. In winter, about half of all sorties involved CCA landings.

One thing that could jam up the carefully managed chaos of cyclic ops was a badly damaged aircraft. A bird inbound with battle damage could necessitate the respotting of the planes on deck, which could result in a scrubbed launch. It was always a judgment call: the captain would have to decide whether the stricken plane could remain airborne long enough so that he could get off the next mission, or whether he should order immediate recovery. Usually he would order the pilot to eject near a rescue ship, but occasionally the pilot was injured or he couldn't safely punch out.

The sustained pace of Rolling Thunder ops was grinding, its effect cumulative. *Essex*-class carriers depleted their magazines in about three days, requiring withdrawal from the firing line to replenish from supply ships. Line periods, supposed to last roughly thirty days before interim rest stops at Cubi, Hong Kong, or other ports, often lasted much longer. The *Oriskany* spent forty-four days on the line in 1969, launching and recovering aircraft flying ninety-minute cycles for twelve or thirteen hours at a time.

World War II pilots would have recognized Rolling Thunders as similar to their armed reconnaissance flights. Instead of specifically briefed targets for a large strike group, tac recces were more often launched against a general area of primary and secondary targets. One day the priority targets might be trucks, another day barges on rivers and canals. Transport and communications routes featured more prominently in Rolling Thunders than anything else, but it was often catch-as-catch-can. In that respect, recces weren't as satisfying for aviators as Alphas, which had a specific goal.

Repeated hunting trips over the beach had one beneficial effect. Aircrews became familiar with the coastal geography of North Vietnam, and most second-tour pilots probably knew the Vietnamese coast better than they did the landmarks around Miramar or Jacksonville. In bad weather, a pilot might discern a minor landmark and know from his position and fuel state whether he should seek a tanker.

From a doctrinal viewpoint, Alphas made more sense than Rolling Thunders. The Alphas enacted the principle of concentration, putting the weight of two carrier air wings, or a navy and an air force strike, on one target complex and saturating the defenses. With time-over-target periods allotted within four or five minutes of one another, coordination was excellent.

Air ops peaked during the one or two days when the relieving carriers arrived on station. Then CTF-77 had as many as four air wings to play with, and mass could be applied if the ROE allowed. The number of stories depended upon the number of serviceable aircraft, and in that respect the simplicity of the two light attack types was most appreciated.

After the propeller-driver A-1 Skyraider was withdrawn in early 1968, *Essex*-class ships bolstered their Skyhawk strength from two A-4 squadrons to three. With an average of fourteen aircraft per squadron, this provided about fifty VA (attack squadron) birds per air wing, and it was a rare day when fewer than forty-five were available. The Skyhawk kept us in the war—its serviceability rate was phenomenal, well over 90 percent.

It was such a simple aircraft that battle damage could often be quickly repaired. One example: the CO of VA-195 in Air Wing 19 sustained a flak hit on his nose section, which jammed the nose-wheel up. The skipper proceeded with a carrier landing using only his mains, skidding down the deck on his nose until the hook stopped him. Two days later, that A-4C was in the air again.

TF 77 lost more Skyhawks than any other type of aircraft, because Skyhawks flew more sorties Up North than any other aircraft. One-third of the navy flights into North Vietnam were by A-4s, which accounted for 38 percent of TF 77 losses. On the other hand, the A-4 had the second lowest loss-to-damage ratio throughout Southeast Asia; only the A-1 was lower. Skyhawks were tough little birds. In a word, survivable.[4]

The next-generation light attack aircraft was Vought's

A-7 Corsair II, bearing a family resemblance to the Crusader. First appearing over Indochina with VA-147 off *Ranger* in December 1967, the A-7A began replacing the A-4 series on most big-deck carriers. With advent of the A-7E, featuring an advanced navigation and bombing system, the Corsair really came into its own. Forward air controllers reported to the *Ranger* and *America* that A-7E bombing accuracy was the best in Vietnam: half the bombs landed within ninety feet of the target, with 90 percent of aircraft systems operational.[5]

Like the A-4, the A-7 was a single-engine, single-seat subsonic aircraft. It wasn't terribly fast, but it was fast enough. Like the Phantom, it was also adopted by the Air Force. Probably the only noteworthy problem encountered with the A-7 program was the rash of losses in spin-related accidents that occurred shortly after the plane joined the fleet. Evaluation determined the Corsair II hadn't been fully spin-tested before entering production, perhaps because of the push to get the new bomber into combat. But the gremlins were exorcised, and A-7 pilots still insist it's a gentleman's airplane.

The navy's round-the-clock bomber was the A-6 Intruder, introduced to combat in the Able model in 1965. It was the other end of the VA spectrum from the A-4/A-7 concept. A two-seat, twin-engine, any-weather electronic marvel, the big Grumman had a lot going for it. Range, payload, and blind bombing were all in its corner; availability was not. A-6 sophistication translated to reduced serviceability rates, and in daylight the Intruder didn't deliver bombs significantly better than A-4s or A-7s, though it did deliver more of them.

On moonless nights and in grim weather (which was frequent), though, the A-6 was the only game in town. It operated solely from big-deck carriers, which normally embarked a twelve-plane squadron. Properly used, the Intruders produced disproportionate results.

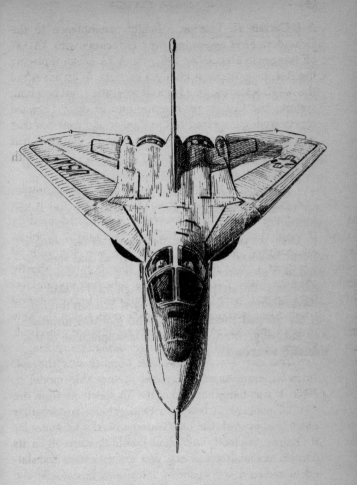

General Dynamics F-111

The *Kitty Hawk* launched two A-6As of VA-85 one April
night in 1966, both headed for the Uong Bi power
plant. Poststrike reconnaissance showed all twenty-six
bombs had landed within the perimeter fence of the
plant. The North Vietnamese concluded that B-52s had
been at work; nothing else was known to deliver under
cover of darkness so intense a bombardment.[6]

A-6 crews have claimed—perhaps with justification—
that their success in flying deep-penetration missions
over rugged terrain prompted the air force to send the
F-111 Up North before it was ready. Although the 111
later became a good airplane, its early loss rate was
prohibitive.

Thus we've seen that the navy's strike warfare
concept balanced simple, reliable aircraft and sophisticated, complex aircraft to provide a full range of mission
capabilities. But despite the very high level of skill and
professionalism demonstrated by naval aviation throughout the Second Indochina War, the tool was misused.
Any lingering bitterness is due to misapplication of this
splendid weapon for so long.

8

PILOT DOWN: SEARCH AND RESCUE, ESCAPE AND EVASION

> *When you're down in the water and the sampans are coming to get you, call an F-4 to pick you up.*
>
> *—Helicopter pilot's retort*

The admirals lost control of the war for a few hours one afternoon in 1968.

A *Ticonderoga* pilot had taken some bad hits and had ejected near Haiphong, landing in the Haiphong River, smack in the middle of Indian country. Floating about two hundred meters from each bank, the flier abandoned his raft when automatic weapons and mortars began ranging in.

A navy helicopter flying toward the downed aviator was itself damaged by gunfire. The chopper pilot pulled back, nursing a stricken aircraft with a dying crewman on board. A second helo arrived, but it too was driven away by intense groundfire.

A line of merchant ships waiting to enter the crowded harbor was anchored a few hundred meters away. Most were Warsaw Pact vessels, and one wonders what tales they told their comrades of that afternoon.

For they witnessed firsthand the value which free men place upon a single life.

The word about the downed pilot had gotten out immediately. Aircraft from all over the Tonkin Gulf raced toward the shootdown site. Someone took control and, with precision born of experience, began to direct attacks upon both banks of the river. AAA came up in awesome volume. SAMs arced into the sky. Aircraft were hit, though none were downed, and the rescue effort continued.

Crusaders, Skyhawks, and Phantoms depleted their ordnance and raced back to their ships. Recovering aboard, they taxied to the catapults for "hot" refueling and arming. Ordnance was loaded, fuel hoses were plugged in, and sometimes a pilot was replaced. The procedure violated every operating technique ever published. It begged for a stray electrical current to set off ordnance. Fortunately, that didn't happen.

Refueled and rearmed—sometimes not even fully loaded—the A-4s and F-8s proceeded at their own frantic pace, oblivious to the ordinary command structure. It had never happened before, and almost certainly it never happened again. But in minutes instead of hours, the Rescue CAP was reinforced, directed by whoever had the picture. A jaygee may have commanded the operation at one point.

The evolution was repeated for hours. Aircraft with bombs or ammunition remaining hustled out to the Gulf for a quick fix from one of the orbiting tankers, then sped back to Haiphong. Probably every sailor in Task Force 77 had his ears tuned to the closest radio or source of scuttlebutt, listening to the drama unfolding one hundred miles away.

Eventually the intensity of the air strikes began to tell. Fire from shore began to slacken, encouraging the duty helicopter to try again. When gunfire erupted once more, the chopper had to withdraw. The aerial pounding resumed. Both banks of the Haiphong River were blasted and smoking as carrier planes arrived overhead, some on their fourth sortie. A few pilots were on their third flight of the day.

Meanwhile, the object of all this attention remained in midstream. The downed pilot drifted in his lifevest and watched the proceedings with strong interest. So far it had been a standoff; the choppers couldn't get to him, but neither could the Vietnamese. Yet it couldn't go on much longer—daylight wouldn't last forever.

Again, the gunfire abated. At that moment, taking advantage of the lull, the helo swooped in. It lowered its hoist, the aviator hooked on and was drawn upward. The helicopter chugged out of that flak-infested hole with one American airman safely aboard.

Word flashed across the task force frequencies: "We got him out!" For the pilots who fought this insane war year after bloody year, this was one victory no one could dispute.

Not all search-and-rescue (SAR) efforts were so successful. In fact, the navy retrieved only about one-sixth of all its fliers known to be down and alive in North Vietnam or adjacent waters.[1] In part, this unimpressive record was due to extrinsic factors: in hostile territory an aroused citizenry spared little effort in snatching "Yankee air pirates," and in addition naval aviators, instinctively heading for the coast when their planes were hit, had to pass over heavily populated and heavily armed Route Packs IV and VI.

But for the most part, the reasons for poor SAR performance were intrinsic, an institutional failure on the part of the navy. When Yankee Team operations began in 1964, the navy possessed no organization dedicated to combat SAR. The navy wasn't alone in this sad situation. The air force, although possessing a SAR force for global operations, did not maintain a wartime search-and-rescue capability beyond 1958. Rescue techniques became standardized, almost rigid, ignoring the differences not only among geographical areas but between peacetime and combat environments as well.[2]

According to one study, combat SAR evolved through a trying series of scrapes. Early experience demonstrated that "combat rescues required more than a crew, a helicopter and good intentions. During this 'dark age of SAR,' men often died attempting a rescue simply because the available crews lacked rescue training and were ignorant of proper recovery techniques. There was a misconception on the part of some helicopter crewmen that rescue entailed nothing more than flying over a downed crewman and picking him up. In each case, problems encountered in mountains, jungles and water pickups required specialization."[3]

Combat SAR abilities remained limited through the early years of the Indochina war. The CIA-operated Air America provided most recovery operations in Laos until well into 1965. The navy tried to alleviate matters— not with helos but with A-1E's rotating through Udorn, Thailand, as SAR escort in 1965. Maintaining four to six Skyraiders away from the task force, however, posed problems. As air operations increased, the A-1s were needed elsewhere, and their limited numbers precluded escort in depth. The air force finally moved in with T28 prop-driven trainers fitted with guns and ordnance, allowing the carrier planes to return to the Gulf.

As the air defenses strengthened in Laos and North Vietnam, combat SAR became increasingly complicated. One or two helos were required, plus A-1s to provide low-level, long-term escort in addition to fighters on CAP and tankers offshore in case the rescue effort became prolonged, as it frequently did. In extreme cases, efforts to retrieve a single pilot or crew might last two or three days.[4]

T-28 Trojan

From 1964 through 1966 the navy's SAR efforts were distributed in remarkably even fashion throughout Indochina. In that thirty-six-month period navy SAR forces rescued sixty-one combat aircrewmen, including nineteen from the Gulf. Another nineteen were picked up in South Vietnam, and eleven were saved in North Vietnam and Laos each. One was fetched back from Thailand. Naturally, the least opposition was encountered over the Gulf, especially away from coastal waters. But the threat levels steadily increased in North Vietnam and Laos, and at least seven navy helos were lost to enemy action through 1967. Sophisticated techniques and sound doctrine brought helo losses down to zero thereafter.[5]

The marked improvement may have been largely due to establishment of a dedicated C/SAR unit. Helicopter Combat Support Squadron Seven (HC-7) was formed with the specific purpose of retrieving downed fliers from enemy territory. HC-7 studied and practiced operational doctrine and techniques and devised appropriate equipment. With HC-7, the navy entered a new era in Combat SAR.

A dozen Sikorsky SH-3As were modified for the

role and sent to various detachments in the Tonkin Gulf. Ordinarily, when an Alpha strike was planned, one helo flew to the northern SAR ship, a destroyer fitted with a helipad, to await developments. A backup chopper was either kept at readiness aboard its carrier or ferried out to the SAR station when the primary helo moved to an orbit point offshore.

Time was crucial in a successful rescue Up North. About three-quarters of all aviators captured by the North Vietnamese were grabbed during their first half-hour on the ground.[6] Therefore, the duty SAR bird positioned itself as close to the target area as it dared.

For strikes west of Hanoi, the air force's Thailand-based squadrons of the Aerospace Rescue and Recovery Service performed nearly all SAR missions. And the blue-suiters fully matched the selfless courage and determination of their navy counterparts. If TF-77 helos fished men out of Haiphong Harbor, the air force "Jolly Green Giants" had their own specialized tasks. One example will suffice.

A Crusader pilot from VF-194 ejected after nursing his badly hit F-8 to a hilly jungle area southwest of "Dodge City"—Hanoi. An ARRS HH-3 arrived on-scene about the same time as a gaggle of NVA soldiers started climbing the hill. It was a race, with the navy flier as the prize.

The HH-3 crew lowered a jungle penetrator on a cable through the triple-canopy foliage. But because of the unusual height of the trees, the penetrator came eight to ten feet short of the pilot's hands, even with the cable fully extended. The Jolly Green was hovering within inches of the treetops when smallarms rounds began tearing into the fuselage. Crewmen were hit, and at least one killed.

That helo pilot had to decide between two very clear alternatives instantly. He could pull up on his collective, adding power and saving his aircraft and crew from further risk. Or he could descend a few feet lower, into the treetops in a heart-pounding, desperate gamble to save that navy pilot from the barbarians on the ground.

The air force driver opted for the save. As he lowered his Sikorsky into the trees the rotor blades started cutting timber, showering the area with wood chips and debris—and rotor tips. With unbalanced blades the HH-3 began vibrating but the helo remained in that tenuous hover long enough for the F-8 pilot to grasp the penetrator sling, hook aboard, and hope for the best.

Now bucking madly, the Jolly Green slowly rose out of the shattered foliage. The swaying was magnified at the end of the cable, and the F-8 pilot banged against tree trunks and limbs all the way up.

There was no way the damaged Sikorsky could clear the area. The pilot had to set down a few miles away in a clearing. But the situation looked considerably better than it had moments before. A reserve Jolly Green was called in, scooped up the survivors, and returned all safely to Udorn.

And to add further insult to the reds, the damaged HH-3 was lifted out that night!

Fixed-wing pilots generally, and jet jockeys particularly, adopted a machoer-than-thou attitude towards helo drivers. After all, it was hard for a "rotorhead" to generate enough speed to really hurt himself, and choppers seemed to adhere to the hang glider's motto: never fly higher than you're willing to fall.

But the Combat SAR folks, bless their torque, were always there when needed. They knew they had a corner on the market, and when some hot jet jock screwed up and found himself staring at a plate of pumpkin soup for dinner, the helos came motoring in at

all of 140 knots to attempt the rescue. They weren't
always successful: sometimes there simply wasn't enough
time, and often the flak was too thick. But the helos had
the last word on the subject. After they'd endured the
slings and arrows of the fast-movers, they'd unzip wry
grins and say, "Yeah, right. Next time you're down in
the water and the sampans are coming to get you, call
an F-4 to pick you up."

There was no arguing with that logic.

Anticipating the worst, most airmen carried personal
weapons. Early in the war, the men in the squadron
ready rooms looked like a Mafia hit team going to work.
Every kind of firearm was carried, depending upon the
individual preference and sense of machismo of the
aviators. There were sawed-off rifles and shotguns,
chopped Thompsons minus stocks, even silenced pistols.
In one extreme example, a fighter pilot scrounged some
grenades from the marines.

Some fliers were more afraid of all those loaded
weapons in the ready room than what awaited them
over the beach. I myself recall a round accidentally
fired in the close, steel confines of the ready room.
The bullet careened about for perhaps five seconds (it
seemed more like five minutes) before expending its
energy.

About 1969 most pilots got rid of their pistols or
loaded them only with flare rounds for signaling. The
most useful piece of survival equipment was the emergency radio (or two if you were smart; battery life was
limited). Two radios and some extra food made much
more sense—a shootout with NVA was almost certainly
a losing proposition.

Yet a couple of instances prove the worth of a
sidearm. One well-known F-8 pilot saved his life with
his issue .38 caliber revolver when shot down near
Thanh Hoa Bridge. Attacked by a machete-wielding

local, the aviator shot the man dead with one well-placed round. Then, seeing a gathering crowd, the flier ejected the remaining rounds from the cylinder. He threw the bullets in one direction and the Smith and Wesson in the other, far into a rice paddy. Then he walked into six years of captivity.[7]

The second episode almost defies belief. In March 1967 an RA-5C off the *Kitty Hawk* was flying a reconnaissance sortie at 350 feet, just off the beach. Making 450 knots, the plane was badly hit from shore and went down in the water. The pilot was killed, but the backseater ejected in time.

The lieutenant (jg) landed on the beach and had waded into the water before being surrounded by numerous locals. He carried the standard issue .38 in a bandolier shoulder holster, but for added safety he left the first two chambers unloaded, using only four rounds in the gun. He also had a .22 automatic under his flight suit.

Thigh-deep in the surf, surrounded by Vietnamese, the NFO knew that resistance was pointless. But he could see the duty SAR helo approaching from the east. He was willing to try something.

One of the Vietnamese removed the .38 from its holster and pointed it at the flier. Another local militiaman covered him with a rifle. The crowd dispersed when A-1s and F-8s from the ResCAP began strafing up and down the beach, suppressing any antiaircraft fire that might impede the rescue.

The airborne pilots could see the three men in the water and adjusted their passes accordingly. They could see that the pilot was covered by two guns, but they couldn't fire at the Vietnamese without risking hitting the American. The most they could do was provide distraction and harassment. That was enough for the cool American in the water. When his potential captors glanced upward, taking in the low-level fly-bys, our man unzipped his flight suit, produced his hideout gun, and instantly chambered a round. With the two locals still distracted, he shot the rifleman in the head: a no-reflex kill. The noise of that .22 round startled the other Vietnamese, who reflexively pulled the trigger of the .38. The hammer fell on an empty chamber, as the Viggie NFO knew it would. He shot the pistol holder, and in seconds he was swimming madly out to sea. The helo swooped in and picked him up.

That story made the rounds through TF 77 and back to Cubi in little longer than it takes to relate the incident. The level-headed flier from "Heavy 13" was assured free drinks at the O Club as long as he was willing to tell his story.

Once a pilot was in the hands of the North Vietnamese, he was destined for prison or worse. In 1966 a senior aviator was shot down north of the DMZ while flying an A-1. His emergency hand-held radio began to beat on "beeper mode," signaling his location. Although there was no voice communication, which was required as standard procedure, most helo crews were willing to attempt a pickup if the possibility seemed remotely worthwhile.

As the H-3 neared the crash site, the NVA opened up. It was a flak trap, a tactic first employed in Laos over a year before. Knowing the Americans would commit aircraft to an attempt, the communists often dangled live bait before the gunners in the form of a downed flier or crew. But this episode had an especially ugly twist.

The badly damaged Sea King barely made if off-shore before going down. After rescue, one of the crewmen reported that just before the NVA opened fire, an enemy soldier had held up the severed head of the Skyraider pilot.

Occasionally a rescue attempt would be called off because losses among helo and ResCAP aircraft (and crews) were too great or too likely. A very attractive idea that kicked around for a while was that of a rescue vehicle that required no crew. A task group commander devised the concept of a helicopter drone as a SAR platform, and it was tested in the fleet. Originally designed as an economical means of tracking or attacking submarines, the helicopter was modified with a long cable attached to a rescue harness. Directed inland by a controller in another aircraft, the drone would be guided to its target by the downed flier himself via radio. The theory was that the remote-controlled helo would be made to hover over the aviator while he snapped into the harness. Then the controller would raise the helo and take it out to sea where the rescue would be completed.

While the contraption was never employed operationally, sentiment in the squadrons remained decidedly skeptical. Few pilots are comfortable riding with other aviators, and the prospects of dangling from a remotely controlled drone were unappealing to many, even in view of the alternative. As one fighter pilot said, "I'd rather eat pumpkin than ride that thing!"

More appealing, from the fliers' viewpoint, was a steerable parachute. With a specially designed canopy, this chute was reported to have a 20- or 30-to-1 glide ratio, which would enable pilots to get away from populated areas. It was still in the developmental stage when the war ended.

Aircrew training included a course in escape and evasion. As events would have it, nobody escaped from a North Vietnamese prison camp to return to American safety, so the proper emphasis belonged upon evasion.

According to doctrine, a downed airman was to hide by day and travel at night. First choice called for getting to the ocean. If one could steal a boat or raft and get far enough into the Gulf, the chance of rescue was very much improved. But evading via the gulf was rarely, if ever, accomplished. On land the prospects for eventual success weren't terrific, but individuals could evade for extremely long times. One air force F-4 pilot survived forty-six days in the jungle before being caught. Another Phantom crewman spent three days overlooking a major MiG base near Hanoi, and duly reported his observations when finally rescued.

While prospects on land were problematical, survival in the water was never a sure thing either. About 30 percent of the aviators who bailed out in the Tonkin Gulf drowned before being picked up.[8]

A signal mirror was the best means of attracting attention. With constant air activity offshore, the odds of being spotted in any daylight period were excellent. Each aircrewman carried such a signal mirror as part of his equipment.

Most fliers were given "blood chits," reminiscent of the famous Chinese nationalist flags sewn on the jackets of the Flying Tigers in World War II. The Vietnam War versions were made of silk cloth, about ten by twelve inches with an American flag and a message in three languages, something to the effect: "I am an American and my government will pay you for my safe return to friendly hands." Each chit was stamped with a serial number, and God help the flier who lost one.

The only people whom fliers were advised to approach were Catholic priests. There were two reasons behind this theory: Catholicism was a widespread religion throughout Indochina. Presumably Catholic priests would be more sympathetic to Americans than most other Vietnamese. Even so, it was considered an extremely risky business, to be attempted only in the direst circumstances.

All U.S. military personnel were instructed in the Code of Conduct, modified after the brutal Korean War experience. Under the code, we were permitted to give only name, rank, date of birth, and serial number. But for an airman, such limitations were absurd. Our carrier aircraft were marked not only with our names but also with the squadron number and ship's name. Most pilots also had unit patches on their flight suits and many flew (against regulations) with wallets in case they were diverted ashore.

The only document we were specially allowed to carry was the Geneva Convention ID card, but the security measures either fell short or were circumvented. I believe the North Vietnamese confronted most new POWs with an almost complete service history. The information came from newspapers, magazines, the *Navy Times*, and ordinary Soviet intelligence data. Occasionally it was augmented by information from American citizens sympathetic to the enemy, though such treasonous actions apparently were never prosecuted. It was that kind of war.

Sensitive tactical data aboard the aircraft generally was destroyed when the ejection seat fired. We especially didn't want the bad guys to get hold of the IFF (Identification, Friend or Foe radar) transponder, and even more important was the communication scrambler that garbled radio transmissions on the discreet frequencies.

After Korea, the air force opened a survival school and navy pilots sometimes attended. They learned survival techniques for polar, jungle, and desert environments. Soon after the Vietnam War started, the navy opened a similar school at Warner Springs, California. All combat aircrew had to attend.

The school had three phases: survival on your own by living off the land (an excellent course); evasion techniques (this lasted two days and was, in my opinion, just so-so); and POW camp indoctrination, which went on for about four days.

This third phase was brutal, and I do not mean "difficult" but grossly harsh. Nowhere else in American military training is a man allowed to *strike* another man; not in the Marine Corps, the SEALs, or the paratroops. I was against it then and I'm against it now. It is not the American way to train people.

A cupped hand was used, and the blow sounded like a rifle shot. On the side of the face the sting was only moderately painful, but sometimes the ear was hit, resulting in a broken eardrum. One of my pilots reported back to the squadron with only a few days until deployment, suffering a broken jaw. Another had frostbite to his feet which lasted between six and eight months.

The "guards" were almost all enlisted sailors of Oriental extraction. They never spoke English to the "prisoners." There were wire fences, gun towers, constant cold, no water, and roll-call formations constantly.

The guards always picked a man—usually a very young enlisted aircrewman—and over those four days completely broke him. He would then sit in a comfortable chair, eating snacks, drinking lots of water and cold beer, with a bemused expression on his face. The purpose was to demonstrate what could be done in only a few days. Needless to say, the young man never went back to a squadron on flight status.

Being without food or water and undergoing constant questioning are useful aspects of training. Most former POWs seem to feel that in that regard the school helped prepare them for their ordeal. But the "training" sometimes went to extremes. Men were sometimes staked to the ground and hosed down at intervals for hours, in winter. Some developed severe chest colds, and there were several cases of pneumonia. Some were placed naked in corrugated aluminum pipes and exposed to the sun for hours. Many "prisoners" were wedged into a confined box, where it was impossible to straighten the legs or back. Limbs went numb, causing adverse aftereffects. Occasionally someone died. One man I knew was kept in the box for about four hours. When he vomited, he choked to death.

Americans have always been able to learn what was required in war without this kind of training. The excesses inflicted upon combat-bound aviators during the Vietnam War originated in the unexpected brutality experienced by POWs in Korea. Now, after two prolonged wars with the communists, we know the nature of the enemy. We needn't repeat the same mistakes again.

In a much lighter vein, a squadronmate and I devised a sure-fire method of "communicating" with a "prisoner" during the Warner Springs portion of Air Wing 19's predeployment training in 1966. Our air wing commander, or CAG, was enduring the none-too-pleasant confines of the simulated POW camp in the hills near San Diego, and Bob McDonough and I resolved to send him a message to boost his morale.

Bob, incidentally, was the original "Maverick," and though he bore little resemblance to Tom Cruise, he had the same sense of fun-loving deviltry that the movie character from *Top Gun* had. Our CAG, widely known as the self-acclaimed World's Greatest Fighter Pilot, had fought the two of us to a draw not long before, and we were out for revenge. The irksome thing about it was that commander Billy Phillips probably *was* the world's greatest fighter pilot. He could do things with a Crusader that had to be seen to be believed. Nobody, but nobody, could outfly him.

Consequently, Maverick and I seized upon our rare

opportunity to even the score. We typed a message to the guards at the training camp and made thousands of copies on VF-191's mimeograph machine. Then we inserted them inside the speed brakes underneath our airplanes, pumping up the brakes by hand from the wheel well.

With the leaflets safely stowed, we manned up and taxied out, trailing stray pieces of paper in our wake. I had the lead, and we made a section takeoff from Miramar.

Though we'd both been "guests" at the POW camp recently, we didn't know exactly where it was. But as luck would have it, we found the compound by flying a sector search based on prominent landmarks we remembered from our own incarceration. We hugged the mountaintops, flying just off the trees at "the speed of heat," intending to surprise the camp with an undetected high-speed approach.

Our tactics almost worked. Later we learned that some guards had spotted us inbound at the last moment and shouted a warning. The air-raid siren blared, and the "captors" yelled for everyone to take cover. CAG Phillips hit his head diving into a shelter and was only vaguely aware of the increasing noise from blank-firing machine guns in the watch towers and the deafening screech of two F-8s streaking directly overhead.

Coming low and fast over the fence, Bob and I popped our speed brakes. The compound was flooded with hundreds—maybe thousands—of our mimeographed leaflets. Then we selected afterburner, honked into vertical climbs, and performed a matched set of aileron rolls to 40,000 feet. We thought CAG Phillips would appreciate a bit of stylish flying.

Only later did we learn the rest of the story. The guards scrambled to pick up all the leaflets so our message wouldn't "contaminate" the criminals confined in the prison. Within minutes the camp loudspeaker blared in a guard's sing-song Oriental voice: "Co-mander Phee-lips, Bee-lee Phee-lips, front and center!"

CAG was promptly paraded before the camp commandant and shown the incriminating evidence. The message stressed our confidence in the CAG. It went something like this:

> Dear Prison Guards:
>   It has come to our attention that you have in your control our beloved air wing commander, Billy Phillips. We feel obliged to inform you that you are wasting your time. You will *never* break that hard-headed, Commie-hating redneck from Tennessee. In fact, he hates *everybody*. He is the toughest SOB in the U.S. Navy and no matter what you try to do to him, he will resist your efforts. The only way you can conquer him is to kill him.
>   Sincerely,
>   Pirate and Maverick

Billy later told us he instantly knew which two idiots were behind the scheme, without even hearing the details. He insisted that we owed him for several lumps he sustained during the subsequent "quiz session."

The prank played upon poor Billy was a high-spirited stunt by a couple of junior officers who truly idolized the man for his exceptional flying ability. As we later learned from survivors of the Hanoi Hilton, little bits of outrageous humor could do much to sustain real POWs in otherwise starkly monotonous circumstances.

9

WHAT IF?

For all sad words of tongue or pen,
The saddest are these: "It might have been!"

—*John Greenleaf Whittier*

Airpower alone could not have won the war in Vietnam, but, properly used, tac air could have prevented the catastrophic loss that ensued when the North Vietnamese Army rolled into Saigon in the spring of 1975. By that time the NVA possessed the strengths and vulnerabilities of a conventional land force. The NVA, in the end, was vulnerable to properly used tac air.

But much earlier than that, the United States, we believe, could have ended aggression from the North. By employing airplanes with conventional weapons in 1965, the United States could have stopped the conflict with small loss of life to Americans and South Vietnamese, and, while the loss Up North would not have been small, it would surely not have approached near the final toll. A properly conducted aerial campaign against the North would be remembered today as a relatively small effort on behalf of a beleaguered people; the Vietnam War would not have developed, as it did, into the gut-wrenching torment of a great nation.

If there is a lingering fallacy about the Second Indochina War, it is that at the tactical level aircraft were ineffective. The myth of airpower's failure has been perpetuated for well over a decade. Let us now examine how aviation should have been brought to bear on the North Vietnamese to have dissuaded them from inciting insurgents in the south.

By the term "airpower" we mean the tactical and strategic employment of conventional aviation ordnance, including air-dropped mines. It is no coincidence that the dramatic change in conditions over Route Packs IV, V, and VI came after the mining of Haiphong and other ports in May 1972.

Mines were under consideration as early as 1965, when carrier-based A-1 squadrons practiced drops in the Philippines.[1] Yet civilian authorities made statements to the effect that mining is an unacceptable act of war. There was talk of potential conflict with Soviet minesweepers. The logic of public servants who regarded the commitment of a half-million men and the most sustained bombing effort in history as *not* acts of war remains impenetrable.

The port of Haiphong could have been neutralized in 1965, as indeed it was seven years later. After issuing warnings for noncombatants to clear the area, we could have destroyed the facilities in one day. North Vietnam would have been left with only the Northeast Railway to China as its primary logistical route, and that rail link could have been cut as repeatedly as necessary. Even if intensive repair work and rugged terrain conspired to keep the rail line functioning, supplies would have merely trickled into North Vietnam.

Mines are weapons that wait. Once they are in place, we don't risk our lives confronting the enemy, and the opposition knows they are there and proceeds only at his own risk. In fact, when Haiphong harbor was finally mined in 1972, no one attempted to get in or out. Thirty-one cargo vessels rode high at anchor for more than eight months—until the "peace" accords were signed. Not only was there personal risk, there was financial risk as well. Lloyds of London had announced a worldwide policy that no vessel incurring mine damage would be eligible for insurance compensation. The intense shipping traffic in and out of Haiphong came to an abrupt halt.

One objection voiced against mining during the 1965–71 period was that mines could easily be swept. But mines are in fact more easily sown than swept. They may be produced in huge quantities and in exceptional variety at moderate cost. In the end, it was U.S. Navy minesweepers that cleared the approaches to Haiphong and other North Vietnamese coastal areas. The North Vietnamese were unable to sweep their own waters because they lacked the capability, for the very good reason that they had had no need to develop that capability during the previous seven years.

The mines were delivered at no loss of American lives. Communist defenses were poorly positioned to engage mining aircraft. No A-6 or A-7 fell to AAA or SAMs while seeding the minefields that morning in May. Yet the nine aircraft involved produced more far-reaching results than had eighty-five hundred aircraft and the seven million tons of ordnance expended throughout Indochina since 1961. Economy of force was never better illustrated.

Even if policy makers accepted the premise that mining was politically impossible in 1965 or shortly thereafter because it endangered Soviet and "neutral" shipping, another option remained. It was more violent and meant immensely greater enemy casualties, but it would at the least have convinced the enemy of our seriousness in defending South Vietnam. That method was unrestricted targeting inside North Vietnam. Instead we chased trucks and barges all over Indochina.

The objective of either mining or bombing North Vietnam was the same: to limit the enemy's capacity for maintaining and supplying large forces in South Vietnam. An old airpower adage holds true: tactical bombing is breaking the milk bottle; strategic bombing is killing the cow. Rather than going after the cow, we tried to break individual bottles—not the most expeditious way of proceeding under the best of circumstances. With a proper targeting policy, we would have been able to interdict enemy transport on a vast scale while bringing immense pressure upon the domestic front, aiming not so much at the enemy's will to fight as at his ability to sustain an offensive in South Vietnam.

This goal was easily within the grasp of tactical airpower, for the North's most vulnerable and potentially most effective target system lay open to attack. We speak of North Vietnam's dikes and dams. North Vietnam has little arable land. What productive land the communists owned was protected by a fragile system of dikes and dams, many of which could have been destroyed in an afternoon. An Alpha launch against a secondary dike system without warning would have provided a valuable bargaining chip early on. Allow the North Vietnamese to absorb the lesson for a day or so, then pose the alternative to them: cease and desist or drown and starve.

The sensitivity of the dikes and dams as targets was recognized by all concerned, including vocal pro-communist elements in the United States.[2] These elements stirred up considerable agitation in insisting that U.S. aircraft were actually bombing such targets when in fact we were not. But the point is clear: the opposition feared that "Yankee air pirates" would actually go after the logical target while those U.S. leaders prosecuting the war devoutly avoided any hint that such a plan was even being considered.

One of the strongest arguments against destruction of the dam system was that such destruction would cause great loss of life among the peasants—"genocide." Americans were somehow expected to refrain from any activity—no matter how logical—that would result in such heavy loss of life and the infliction of hardship upon an enemy civilian population. Yet such a viewpoint overlooked the essential reality of twentieth-century warfare. The strategic bombing campaigns of World War II were for the most part directed against civilians. It has been said that there are few civilians left in the world. Certainly in any industrialized nation, a large segment of the population is devoted wholly to supporting the military–armament industry. And in a socialized country such as North Vietnam, a good many peasants were engaged in supporting the war effort by producing food.

The cost to North Vietnam as the result of unrestricted targeting could probably have run into the millions of dead and displaced people. But on the other hand, if faced with the prospect of such devastation, would the hard-eyed men in Hanoi have persisted with their mischief in the south?

With these two exceptions, mining Haiphong harbor and destroying dikes and dams, most of the other options open to American arms were acted upon. Later we did mine the harbor, but that came very late. Now we are considering the "what ifs" of 1965–66. What actions could we or should we have taken to end the war early? A look at a map tells us of one option. With growing troop strength in South Vietnam, a mighty fleet offshore, and outright ownership of the sky, the United States could have exercised one operation that it performs better than anyone else. Consider Korea in the fall of 1950, and how the Inchon landing reversed a drastically worse situation than existed in 1965–66 Vietnam. Consider North Vietnam's geography—its long, exposed coastline—and its supply system to the south. Consider what combined arms—airpower coupled with seapower—can do to conventional forces responding to a landing. Consider the amphibious option.

Churchill once stated, with precise understanding, that negotiating with communists was simply getting them to agree to stop doing to you what you're not doing to them. In Vietnam, the Viet Cong and NVA were widely active in the South, but had no worry of reciprocal action being taken in the North. A limited-objective invasion of North Vietnam, perhaps a two-pronged thrust from across the DMZ and from the Tonkin Gulf into Route Packs I and II, would have had several benefits. First, it would have forced an immediate shift in the enemy's attention from the South to its own territory. That in turn would have required redistribution of troop strength, if in fact those formations in the South could make their way back through the new allied perimeter.

Second, to respond to such a move the North Vietnamese Army would have had to come into open battle, a condition so long sought in vain in the South. And when the NVA engaged, American superiority in combined arms would prove decisive. Airpower, sea-borne artillery, and maneuverability are all elements of the military doctrine inherent to the Navy–Marine Corps way of making war. Yet these elements were either lacking or misapplied in the ensuing seven years.

For either military or political reasons, Hanoi could hardly have ignored an invasion in its southern territory. But even if Hanoi had refused to commit its forces to the contest, we would have retained a major advantage. With stop-lines well defined, the United States and South Vietnam would have possessed a tremendous bargaining chip in a high-stakes real estate game. Withdrawal of NVA forces and logistical support for the VC in the South would have been the price for return of a sizable chunk of North Vietnam.

Third, seizure of enemy territory would have gone a long way toward severing important supply lines to the north. Granting allowance for that portion of the Ho Chi Minh Trail that detoured westward into Laos, the results would still have been felt.

President Johnson's avowal of "no wider war" apparently prohibited the full application of naval assets, although senior Marine Corps officers strongly argued for a seaborne invasion as the best means of forcing Hanoi to negotiate. The "no wider war" statement may have been aimed not only at American citizens but also, perhaps especially, at the Chinese communist leadership in Peking. But how realistic was the potential for massive Chinese intervention? If Korea was any example, not until total capitulation was pending would the Chinese have committed themselves. A case can be made that stop-lines in southern North Vietnam would have helped bring about in a timely fashion a negotiated settlement to the hostilities, thereby gutting the chance that China would have entered the war at all.

Implementation of all or a combination of the three options outlined here—early mining, unrestricted bombing of dams and dikes, and amphibious invasion—would probably have shortened the war and produced an outcome more in line with American and South Vietnamese visions of the future. Airpower would have played a significant part in any option.

While airpower alone would not have brought the Indochina conflict to a satisfactory conclusion, airpower alone has twice gained major foreign policy goals for the

United States. The first occasion was in 1948–49 when the Berlin Airlift kept that city supplied despite a Soviet blockade. The intention of the U.S. government at the time was to sustain the population of West Berlin despite Soviet interference. Airlift was the sole means of circumventing the problem, and it succeeded.

The second occasion was during the Vietnam War and actually consists of two parts, about eight months apart. In May 1972, the mining operation cut off from the communists their primary source of military supplies. The bargaining which ensued was largely a result of that action, and when the North Vietnamese again proved recalcitrant in Paris, the B-52 strikes against Hanoi and Haiphong quickly brought things to a conclusion.

What was possible in 1972, against the most experienced air-defense network on earth, certainly was possible in 1965–66 against an embryonic defense. Aviation, mated with proper doctrine and professional application, can accomplish a great deal. In concert with sustained strategy and combined arms, it can lead to military success in war. Perhaps more important, the

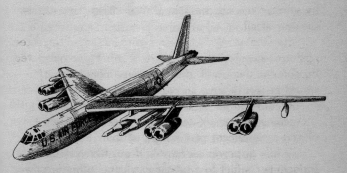

B-52

threat of airpower linked to the perceived belief that it will be employed can accomplish nearly as much at little cost to either side. Forty years of nuclear deterrence is an example on a global scale.

Aircraft, like anything else, possess certain advantages and shortcomings. We have touched upon the former. Among the latter are the obvious: airplanes can neither seize nor hold ground. They cannot defeat an enemy who refuses to concentrate. They cannot sustain a government lacking wisdom or resolve.

But *what if* airpower had been properly employed in Vietnam? Would we have lost 56,000 American lives? Would an eight-year struggle have nearly destroyed the American economy and public confidence in government? Would American institutions have suffered long-term political damage? Would all of Vietnam, Laos, and Cambodia now live under communism?

Perhaps intelligent use of airpower would have made no difference. Perhaps the result would have been the same. But the evidence implies otherwise.

Sadly, the philosophy and doctrine that brought success in Korea was ignored in Vietnam. Authors of navy and air force histories correctly analyzed the rudiments of success in dealing with Asian communism well before the Second Indochina War. Their words are haunting. The official air force historian summarized:

> During World War II U.S. Air Force officers had learned that airpower could most effectively destroy an enemy's capacity to fight by strategic air attacks against his sources of production. The Communist ground forces in Korea, however, drew most of their logistical support from sources outside Korea which could not be attacked. In view of the situation [American airpower could only] interdict the

lines of communication supporting the North Korean Army. To achieve the best results, any interdiction campaign had to be *well planned as to objectives and persistently sustained in its execution*.[3] [Emphasis added.]

In the naval history of the Korean War, Vice Admiral C. Turner Joy, naval theater commander in Korea in 1950 and 1951 and chief of the United Nations truce delegation team, stated:

> During the last ten months of my tour in the Far East I was fortunate, or unfortunate, enough to face our common enemy across the conference table. If there are still those in the Free World who believe that the enemy can be moved by logic, or that he is susceptible to moral appeal, or that he is willing to act in good faith, those remaining few should immediately disabuse themselves of that notion. It was a mistake to assume, or even hope, that the enemy was capable of acting in good faith. Future textbooks can set down the maxim that *the speed with which agreement is reached with the communists varies directly as the military pressure applied, and that the worth of any agreement is in proportion to the military strength you are able and willing to apply to enforce it.*[4] [Emphasis added.]

Ironically, it was the destroyer bearing his name that was involved in the Tonkin Gulf incident of August 1964.

Less than a dozen years had passed between the end of the war described in these two statements and commencement of large-scale U.S. operations in Vietnam. That so obvious a lesson should be lost in so short a time is at once pitiful and amazing.

But more to the point, a similar span of years has now elapsed since the end of Vietnam.

10

RECOMMENDATIONS

The lessons of the Vietnam War are legion. They range from the obvious, "Don't fight unless you mean to win," to "Only one pass at a defended target." The following are a handful of what the authors believe are the most important and attainable objectives for naval aviation. Briefly, they may be summarized as people, planes, and procedures.

People are the most important part of any organization, at once its greatest strength and potential weakness. The degree to which an organization succeeds or fails largely depends upon leadership, motivation, and expertise in depth—up and down the line. The unit or armed service as a whole may possess some exceptional leaders, a handful of highly motivated individuals, or a few skilled performers. But unless those qualities exist in quantity, the outlook is bleak.

In short, an air force—especially a naval air force— is a fragile weapon. It must be constantly exercised— maintained at a high state of operational readiness with a uniformly high skill level. The loss of a few leaders should not detract significantly from the stock of motivational talent. But frequently such losses cause greater harm. Situations existed during Vietnam in which aircrew casualties could not be replaced, and some squadrons found themselves in the astonishing position of receiving extra aircraft but no new pilots.

Attrition, whether due to operational, combat, or rotational causes, easily can blunt the air weapon's sharp edge. In aviation more than perhaps any other endeavor, quality people are essential to long-term success. Experience, combined with skill and motivation, may be enhanced or lost according to personnel availability. Gone are the days of World War II when aviators were produced in tens of thousands. No more may we send pilots into combat with 450 flying hours—200 in type—with perhaps only two dozen carrier landings. The equipment and the threat level will not permit it.

The first task of air leaders must be to ensure a continuing source of competent aircrews and commanders at the tactical level. But there are other tickets to be punched along the way. Staff duty, schools, and other "career-enhancing" slots must be obtained. These postings usually have little to do with preparing to fight air war at sea, but they are important professional steps for careerists.

One of the manifestations of the situation is a relatively poor retention rate. The figures rise and fall, according to the civil aviation job market, but in 1986 the navy was short eleven hundred pilots. There is an oft-cited reason for this; it comes under the heading of "job satisfaction."

Hundreds of aviators—good, experienced fliers— leave the service annually. If their attitude could be collectively paraphrased, it would sound like this: "Hey, I don't want to be CNO. I just want to fly the airplane."

It needn't be that way. Commercial aviation has much to offer a pilot: good pay, more time with one's family, and the opportunity to settle down in one place. But it can never offer the challenge, the excitement and the satisfaction of carrier aviation. The carrier environment, the exotic equipment, the use of ordnance combine to overwhelm—to our thinking, at least—whatever attractions the airlines might hold. It is incumbent upon the navy to dangle those riches—carriers, high-performance planes, and ordnance—in the most enticing manner possible.

The navy could retain more aviators by allowing them to be purely and simply—aviators. No ticket-punching, no staff slots, no "career-enhancing" assignments. The pure aviator's career would be purely *flying*, period.

Steps have been taken in this direction. The limited-duty officer (LDO) aviator program is giving way to the aviation duty office (ADO), aimed at pilots who are not oriented toward squadron command or flag rank. They will not be selected for staff billets or service colleges but can be retained on active duty thirty years or more. This is heartening news and could do much to attract and—more important—retain experienced, motivated aviators. When announced, however, the ADO program was expected to produce only about 650 individuals over a five-year period. That rate of advance probably would not fill the gap.

Still, establishment of an exclusive (as opposed to a limited-duty) aviator slot should accomplish several things. It could build a cadre of highly trained and experienced pilots and aircrew. In exchange for, say, twenty years in the air, these fliers accept the knowledge that their career would probably peak at commander and that they would never screen for command.

Unrealistic? Consider the thousands of Reserve aviators and maintenance personnel now on the roster. Reserve squadrons typically are topheavy with lieutenant commanders who know there is little prospect for achieving command status because there are too many people for the available slots. But that's in no way bad.

Quite the contrary. The very fact that the "problem" exists means that all those folks are happy with their work. They like to fly, they enjoy the navy community, and generally they put in more time than is required. In short, they're motivated.

There is no reason to suppose that the same type of individual would not be attracted by permanent flying status in the regulars. As long as he can pass the flight physical and can fly the airplane, he's assured of doing the one thing on earth he wants to do. That's a powerful attraction for any field of endeavor.

In exchange, the navy would gain an invaluable increase in operational readiness and expertise. Tactical proficiency would grow, and our air weapon would be far less vulnerable to moderate attrition.

Nor should we limit this offer to commissioned pilots. Many aircrew slots that now require officers can certainly be filled by enlisted personnel. From a practical viewpoint, a college diploma is no more essential to operating avionics than it is to flying a military aircraft. Aircrew positions in ECM and ASW squadrons have been ably filled in the past— as some are today—with noncommissioned personnel. Opening nonpilot duties to enlisted personnel would provide at least two direct benefits in morale and monetary terms.

One of the problems in Vietnam was that the enlisted maintenance and flight-deck troops had little interaction with aircrew. Aviators were officers, and regardless of how good the command relationship, a line existed between the aviator-officers and the maintenance-enlisted. If enlisted fliers had been able to go over the beach on a daily basis, either to drop bombs or blast electrons, the hard-working men in the air wing and ship's company would have a greater share in the endeavor. The ages-old line between officer and enlisted would have blurred a little: a good thing.

Grumman F-14A Tomcat

A more tangible benefit is the financial one. It costs less, both in salary and retirement expenses, to place enlisted people in aircrew slots. This point alone should make an impression upon a budget-conscious Congress.

In addition to quality people, the navy needs quality aircraft. In particular, it needs a high-performance, low-cost fighter. It has not possessed such an airplane since the F-8, despite protestations that may arise from the F-14 and F-18 communities. The Tomcat and the Hornet, good as they are, have two strikes against them: they are multipurpose aircraft—a fighter-interceptor and fighter-bomber, respectively—and they are very expensive. Depending upon accounting methods, the unit cost of a Tomcat or Hornet runs between twenty and thirty-five million dollars.

At those prices, no nation can afford to lose very many airplanes. A low-cost, high-performance fighter would not replace the F-14 or F-18, rather it would augment those two designs. The F-14 and F-18 would still perform their functions of fleet defense and strike missions.

The dual-purpose fighter-bomber ("strike fighter" in today's parlance) is an attractive concept, but it contains a hidden flaw. No matter how good the airplane or how reliable, the human factor will compromise combat effectiveness. Assuming a new design is capable of performing the aerial combat and air-ground missions equally well, no pilot will master both jobs with equal proficiency. Training time is too limited and too expensive for facility in two such dissimilar roles. The problem was evident in the FA-18 program very early, and attack pilots expressed concern that they would not receive enough flight hours in air-to-air combat to enable themselves to be fully "self-escorting." That situation has not been remedied, nor is it likely to be. Naval aviation's leadership decided—quite correctly—that VA pilots would receive priority training in attack missions. Fighter pilots would emphasize air combat.

In some situations, the self-escorting strike aircraft would work well. Third-world opponents or outnumbered adversaries could probably be handled by strike-fighter pilots with moderate ACM experience. But surely nobody will suggest that we prepare for less than top-notch enemies. If we reach the point of engaging world-class opponents in a contest for aerial supremacy, more than likely *we* will be outnumbered. Then we must truly field the first team.

That means dedicated fighter pilots who plan for, practice, and think nothing but fighter combat. It means, perhaps, the limited-duty aviator lured by the offer of twenty years in the cockpit with no career interruptions away from the tactical level, other than Training Command.

And it means a first-line fighter aircraft designed

and armed with just one mission in mind: engaging and defeating enemy fighters in the air. For without such a capability, airpower is compromised. All other functions of which aircraft are capable—strike, reconnaissance, and surveillance—stem from air superiority.

We require a fighter that is affordable and that can be produced in relatively large numbers, for the sad fact is that planes are lost not only in combat but in training sessions too. If we are to train fighter pilots to peak capacity, we need a design that can absorb the operational and training losses that are inevitable in pushing the outside of the envelope. Aviation safety is fine and desirable, but not at the expense of combat preparedness. We have already seen that such a philosophy pays huge combat dividends—witness the F-8 community of the late 1950s to mid-1960s.

The fighter I envision would follow classical design: a single-seat, probably single-engine plane no larger than necessary to accommodate the internal fuel tanks required for, say, four hundred nautical miles. That means a clean-wing design capable of in-flight refueling and unencumbered by hard-points upon which bombs can be hung. This, rather than any engineering criterion, will be the most difficult specification to meet; budgeteers and politicians loathe a single-purpose flying machine. But these people never pay the price for failure in combat.

Armament would be basic but ample: heat-seeking missiles and an internal gun with as many rounds as shrewd engineering can manage. I would include no radar missiles and consequently the aircraft would have none of their weight nor be burdened with complex systems. Lest this seem overly simple, stop a moment to consider the evolution of air combat since Vietnam.

Increasing sophistication and its attendant cost have yielded minimal combat benefits. In the final phase of the Vietnam War, twenty-three of twenty-four navy MiG kills were made by Sidewinders, not by Sparrows. Reports from the Middle East indicate that the eminently successful Israeli Air Force relies far more upon guns and 'winders than upon Sparrows. In clear air, with visual identification possible (and probably required by the rules of engagement), the long-range weapons are often superfluous.

We already have the ultimate stand-off missileer in the F-14, capable of both Sparrow and Phoenix engagements at extreme ranges. Thus, our cut-and-thrust dogfighter requires no duplication of radar missile armament. Send the specialists over the beach to clear the air of opposing aircraft, retaining the Tomcats and Hornets for fleet defense, strike, and reinforcement if needed. Should tactics require, integrated formations of missileers and gunfighters can be developed.

The clear-air mass gunfighter, long proclaimed defunct, would in fact be useful to us now and in the future. As countermeasures grow more effective, radar-guided missiles and their tracking systems become more vulnerable. Radar can be spoofed, and even heat-seeking missiles can be decoyed by flares. Consequently, we may be entering an era in which sophistication has turned around on itself, and the "dumb" weapon may prove the most effective. A bullet, after all, may not be smart, but neither can it be deceived.

The fighter described here would be somewhere between the F-16 and the F-20 in size, cost, and configuration. An affordable dogfighter is one not only low in unit price but which can be procured in sufficient numbers so that training losses are more easily absorbed than at present. It is a sign of the times that a ten-million-dollar airplane may be considered "cheap," but surely American industry can produce a competitive fighter for one-half to one-third the cost of current, more complex aircraft. Shifting funds from current programs to the new fighter program would be another way of achieving the often-discussed but seldom-achieved "high-low mix." If we decide to augment current types with the new fighter, obviously we do not need as many of the more costly designs.

The number of fighters required to achieve and sustain air superiority may depend upon that equation, whether with a new airplane or a carrier-modified variant of an existing one. In either case, history and logic insist upon such consideration.

We have touched upon the first two of the "Three Ps": people and planes. Now let us examine a procedure that can enhance the combat capability of naval aviation.

This procedure is easily obtained. The navy needs an institutional memory, a means of assessing and disseminating tactical doctrine. In the course of each new war, carrier fleet squadrons found themselves rediscovering basic truths: you don't make multiple passes at a defended target; you don't fly low into a target area where your aircraft are easily hit by smallarms or automatic weapons; you don't rely on your training in fleet air defense to support you in fighter-versus-fighter combat. The list could go on.

Yet only ten years after the air war ended above North Vietnam, U.S. Navy squadrons were committing the same errors and suffering the same unnecessary losses as characterized the war in 1964–65. The retaliatory strike against Syrian SAM batteries in Lebanon in December 1983 lost two aircraft: one pilot dead and another flier a POW. The cause: too long in the target area and multiple passes.

Ironically, in terms of institutional memory, naval aviation started well. By 1943 the Bureau of Aeronautics had established a monthly tactical circular for distribution to all fleet squadrons and issued an extremely detailed, well-designed, after-action document. Form ACA-1 remains a model forty years later. It could be reprinted and distributed today with remarkably little alteration. Interested parties are referred to the Operational Archives Branch of the Navy History Office in the Washington Navy Yard.

Tactical procedures were generally good in Korea, owing in large part to the high percentage of World War II aviators still on active duty. But documentation and after-action reporting showed a notable decline. Twenty-odd years later, in Southeast Asia, the situation had worsened to the point of neglect. Peacetime procedures, born of a peacetime mentality, led to disproportionate losses during the 1964–65 operations against an air defense network that should have been conquered at a fraction of the cost.

As the opposition gained experience and benefited from our own ROE, Task Force 77 air wings also learned hard lessons. By the end of a Tonkin Gulf tour, aircrews were battlewise and cagey—such is the process of operational evolution. They had learned how to adjust to an ever-changing defense.

But when the air wing rotated home, it was often replaced by squadrons entering combat for the first time. There was no memory to draw upon, no information passed on to ease the transition. Consequently, the same painful lessons were learned again and again—for about eight years.

Perhaps it could be argued that a requirement for recording experiences should have existed in the office of the Chief of Naval Operations, but it did not. In fact, from the mid to late 1950s, unit reporting was officially curtailed. And when unit reporting was reinstituted, only annual accountings were required. Useful detail was lacking.

Operational reporting and standard doctrine could have been instituted at any intervening level: CinCPac, AirPac and AirLant, TF 77 or the CarDivs. Even at the air wing level. But apparently no such action was taken, much to the detriment of the U.S. Navy when war came.

In 1984 naval aviation took a landmark step in establishing the Strike Warfare Center at NAS Fallon, Nevada. "Strike University" is responsible for originating and disseminating doctrine, while training not only aircrews but strike leaders and planners as well. The results have been proven in combat, as shown by the success of two 1986 operations against Libya. The contrast between Lebanon in 1983 and Libya three years later could hardly be more dramatic. In the latter case, more aircraft operated in a higher threat level for longer periods, without loss. "Strike U" and the renaissance of tactical thought in naval aviation had made the difference.

One possible addition might enhance naval aviation's institutional memory. The navy should consider establishing a tactical board with permanent status at CNO level. The board would be composed of both active-duty and retired aviators, preferably with combat experience and a familiarity with current equipment. Thousands of qualified men are available, many of whom would jump at the chance to continue making a contribution to navy air.

The board's purpose would be twofold: first, review tactical doctrine where it exists and examine it in light of combat experience; and second, help formulate tactical doctrine that reflects combat experience.

This would not involve running operations by remote control—we tried that in Vietnam and it failed. Rather, the board's recommendations would be the basis of operating procedures and tactics, to be altered as necessary at the tactical level. Since Strike University is responsible for such considerations, the board could perhaps work jointly with the Fallon complex. What we seek—however it is achieved—is accountability. A squadron or wing commander who loses aircraft because he ignored sound doctrine should be held to account.

Our tactical board should be constituted in a way that enables the broadest, most efficient dissemination of its work. Current operational analysis often is theoretical or published beyond the realm of fliers and shooters. The major benefit of a tactical board composed of combat-experienced aviators is that it forms a bridge across the gap between theory and practice. Ten years after Vietnam, perhaps 5 percent of fleet aviators possessed combat experience. Sometimes it takes a man who has been shot at to best evaluate weapons and tactics. True, the weapons grow more sophisticated, the tactics more complex, but the nature of combat does not change. Two things seem eternal: no plan survives contact with the enemy, and nothing is true in tactics. We could benefit from continuing reference to those who have learned the lessons first-hand.

At the very least, a devil's advocate is needed to question the conventional wisdom, to ask "stupid questions," to play the man from Missouri: "Show me." No such method existed before Vietnam, and those "what if" questions were never asked.

This is not to say we assume automatically that combat procedures in World War II, Korea, or Vietnam would hold consistent in the increasingly sophisticated and complex aerial arena of the late twentieth century. Military history shows it is an error to think the next war will resemble the last. Nevertheless, yesterday's aircrews can lend knowledge and perspective to today's warriors, and where they can, they should. The procedures for them to do so should be put in place. Conceivably, such knowledge could make a difference one day in the Indian Ocean, in the North Atlantic, or in the Mediterranean.

APPENDIX A

VIETNAM AIR WAR CHRONOLOGY, EMPHASIZING NAVAL AVIATION

1964

May	Yankee Team operations begin with navy and air force recon flights over Laos.
June 6	An RF-8 becomes the navy's first aircraft loss, over Laos. The pilot was captured by communist forces but escaped.
August 2	North Vietnamese PT boats attack destroyer *Maddox*.
August 4	North Vietnamese PT boats reportedly attack *Maddox* and *Turner Joy*.
August 5	Carriers *Ticonderoga* and *Constellation* launch sixty-four aircraft against enemy PT boat bases in Operation Pierce Arrow. Two planes are shot down, one pilot killed and one captured.
August 7	Congress passes the Tonkin Gulf Resolution.
	Photorecon flights begin over North Vietnam.
	Phuc Yen Airfield (Hanoi) receives thirty-six MiG-15 and -17 fighters.
October 23	Navy aircraft begin providing cover for Laotian government forces.
November	Soviet intelligence-gathering ships arrive off Guam.
December 14	Barrel Roll flights (armed recon) begin over southern Laos.

1965

Early	Bullpup guided bomb (AGM-12) reported in use.
February 8	American and South Vietnamese aircraft attack enemy barracks and facilities at Dong Hoi, North Vietnam, in Operation Flaming Dart.
February 11	Flaming Dart II proceeds with additional attacks in North Vietnam's panhandle in response to enemy actions in South Vietnam.
February 13	President Johnson authorizes Operation Rolling Thunder, air strikes against North Vietnam.
March 1	Rolling Thunder begins.
March 3	Operation Blue Tree commences: medium-level photo-recon and damage-assessment flights over North Vietnam.
April	North Vietnamese electronics capabilities increase.
	SA-2 SAMs are detected southeast of Hanoi. Radar homing and warning equipment is added to reconnaissance U-2s.
	The air force deploys EB-66 electronic countermeasures aircraft to Southeast Asia.
April 3	Extended Barrel Roll operations, called Steel Tiger, are conducted by navy aircraft in the Laotian panhandle.
	MiG-17s shoot down two F-105s in the first conclusive air combat of the war.
April 5	An RF-8 photographs a SAM site under construction, but such targets remain immune for nearly four months.
April 9	In an engagement with Chinese communist MiG-17s south of Hainan, VF-96 loses an F-4B while claiming a MiG.
April 10	A Joint Chiefs plan for Rolling Thunder is proposed with an Alpha section containing major fixed targets. Thus originates the term "Alpha strike."
April 15	Carrier aircraft bomb Viet Cong positions in the Black Virgin Mountains of South Vietnam.

May	The first carriers are deployed to Dixie Station off South Vietnam.
May 13	Air operations against North Vietnam are suspended.
May 18	Rolling Thunder resumes.
May 25	The Soviets announce construction of SAM sites around Hanoi.
June 5	Five carriers are on station in the Tonkin Gulf. Full-time staffing of Dixie Station begins, 90° 30'N, 108°E.
June 17	In the navy's first decisive aerial combat of the war, two VF-21 F-4Bs destroy two MiG-17s with Sparrow missiles.
July	The A-6 Intruder begins combat operations in Rolling Thunder. VA-75 off *Independence* inaugurates the new bomber to combat.
July 24	An air force F-4 becomes the first plane downed by an SA-2.
July 27	First strike against a SAM site.
August	Chinese antiaircraft units begin operating in North Vietnam.
	First Iron Hand (anti-SAM) strikes result in many losses among attacking aircraft.
September	First strikes into Route Pack VI, the Hanoi–Haiphong area.
October 17	First successful Iron Hand mission against a SAM site.
November	Security measures are taken to limit the amount of electronic intelligence available to Soviet ships off Guam, where B-52 Arc Light missions are launched.
December 22	The first industrial targets are attacked in North Vietnam.
December 25	The Johnson Administration halts bombing with the intention of beginning peace talks.

1966

December 26	Air operations resume in South Vietnam and Laos.
January 4	North Vietnam describes the bombing halt as a U.S. trick.
January 31	Rolling Thunder resumes against southern North Vietnam.
February	The navy is assigned Route Packs II, III, IV, and VI-B.
March	Shrike (AGM-45) antiradiation missiles are introduced to combat against SAM-guidance radars.
March 5	General Maxwell Taylor advocates mining Haiphong Harbor.
	First use of an Alpha section in a Rolling Thunder order. Provision for Alphas had been made eleven months before.
April	Yankee Station is moved northward.
April 12	First B-52 missions into North Vietnam.
April 19	Navy planes strike the coal port of Cam Pha, thirty-five miles from the China border.
April 23	U.S. aircraft encounter MiGs in strength.
May	Alpha strikes are flown into Route Pack VI.
June 29	Two new target systems are authorized and attacked: major industries in northeastern North Vietnam, and the country's entire petroleum-oil-lubricant (POL) system.
Summer	Shrikes are fired against enemy Fansong and Firecan radars.
	ECM equipment—navy ALQ-51 and air force ALQ-71—is used against SA-2's Fansong B radar.
	Cluster bomb units (CBU-24, -29, and -49) become available.
August 5	The Soviets protest damage to a Russian ship.
August 28	The Soviets announce they are training NVAF pilots.

November	The U.S. military command establishes coordination and control of all air operations throughout Indochina.
December	First air strikes near Hanoi.
December 25–26	The United States conducts a forty-eight-hour stand-down for Christmas.

1967

January 1	Another forty-eight-hour stand-down for observance of New Year.
January 2	Operation Bolo results in seven MiG kills by air force F-4Cs, the biggest air battle to date.
February 13	President Johnson initiates a six-day bombing halt while Soviet Premier Kosygin visits London.
February 26	Mining begins on five North Vietnamese waterways, completed by mid-April.
March	The Walleye optically guided missile (AGM-62) is initiated into combat in an attack on Sam Lon barracks.
March 10	First attack against Thai Nguyen steel and iron works.
April 20	U.S. aircraft attack powerplants in Haiphong for the first time.
April 27	Navy aircraft strike Kep Airfield and USAF planes attack Hoa Lac Airfield.
May	Routine Alpha strikes begin in North Vietnam.
May 20	Military targets in downtown Hanoi are attacked.
May 23	A ten-mile no-bombing circle is placed around Hanoi.
June	MiGs withdraw to Chinese bases.
June 17	Rail targets near Hanoi are struck in the heaviest air attacks in nine months.
July 29	A flight-deck fire aboard *Forrestal* kills 132 men.
August	A two-month restriction is placed on all targets in central Hanoi, effective to October.
	The air force conducts the first strike against the Paul Doumer bridge.

August 30	A bombing effort to isolate Haiphong continues with strikes against road, rail, and canal traffic.
September 11	Navy planes hit port facilities in Cam Pha for the first time.
October	Operation Sea gap begins, collecting guidance and fusing data on Fansong radars from ships in the Tonkin Gulf.
October 8	First strike against Cat Bi airfield near Haiphong.
October 25	First strike against Phuc Yen, North Vietnam's largest airfield.
November 16	First air strikes against Haiphong shipyards.
November 17	First air strike against Bac Mai airfield near Hanoi.
December 4	A-7A Corsair IIs introduced to combat by VA-147 from *Ranger*.
December	North Vietnam rejects President Johnson's five-point peace plan.

1968

January	North Vietnamese AN-2s stage bombing raids into Laos and fly night missions against South Vietnamese vessels.
	The Russians protest bomb damage to a Soviet ship in Haiphong Harbor and the Johnson Administration says it will make every effort to avoid a repetition.
January 23	North Korea seizes the U.S. intelligence-gathering ship *Pueblo*.
January 30	Communist forces launch the Tet offensive, beginning a seventy-seven-day seige at Khe Sanh and instigating fighting in every large city in South Vietnam.
March	U-2 and SR-71 fights cover South Vietnam and Laos, and North Vietnam, respectively.
	Air strikes against North Korea in retaliation for the *Pueblo* incident are planned, then cancelled.
	Lyndon Johnson announces he will not run for reelection.

April 3	Bombing of North Vietnam is further restricted to only the area south of the 19th Parallel.
May	Standard Antiradiation Missile (AGM-78) is used against SA-2 and AAA sites.
	Electronic intelligence-gathering aircraft are deployed in Southeast Asia.
	Despite a rift between Hanoi and Peking, the Chinese continue to operate radar sites in North Vietnam.
June 5	North Vietnam demands an unconditional end to U.S. bombing.
September	Rockeye bombs and EKA-3 ECM/tankers are introduced.
September 19	An F-8C of VF-111 scores what was to be the last MiG kill until March 1970.
November 1	Rolling Thunder is suspended as the Johnson Administration halts bombing throughout North Vietnam.
November 6	Richard Nixon wins the presidential election, defeating Hubert Humphrey.

1969

Early	Air Force planes use the Paveway laser-guided bomb for the first time.
June 8	President Nixon meets President Thieu of South Vietnam and announces a troop reduction of twenty-five thousand in South Vietnam by September.
August 4	First meeting between Henry Kissinger and the North Vietnamese delegation in Paris.
September 3	Ho Chi Minh dies. North Vietnam reestablishes relations with Peking. POW treatment also improves.
December	Enemy Fansong radars are modified to permit earlier SAM arming, improving low-altitude effectiveness.

1970

March 5	Confirmation of SA-2 deployment in Laos.
March 28	An F-4J of VF-142 shoots down a MiG-21, the only aerial kill of the 1969–71 period.
April 30	American troops begin a two-month drive into Cambodia to cut enemy supply routes and uproot Viet Cong headquarters.
May	The Nixon Administration announces that recent air strikes into North Vietnam are larger than any since 1968. Primary targets are communications and air-defense facilities.
October	President Nixon proposes an in-place ceasefire. Hanoi rejects the proposal and demands American withdrawal.
November 22	A well-executed attempt to rescue POWs at Son Tay, deep in North Vietnam, fails because prisoners had been moved days earlier. Large air raids are conducted as part of an elaborate diversion.

1971

Entire year	Many protective reaction strikes are conducted against SAM and AAA batteries firing upon U.S. recon aircraft.
December 26	Operation Proud Deep Alpha begins, involving five days of air strikes in three North Vietnamese provinces below 20°N.

1972

Early	Protective reaction strikes increase. The optically guided Walleye II glide-bomb is introduced.
January 19	The VF-96 team of Cunningham and Driscoll scores the first MiG kill in nearly two years, flying an F-4J off *Constellation*.

January 23	SA-3s are suspected to be operational in North Vietnam.
March 19	American aircraft record their one hundredth protective reaction strike.
March 30	North Vietnam opens its massive spring offensive across the Demilitarized Zone into South Vietnam.
April	A new surface threat appears as the SA-7 heat-seeking missile is deployed in North Vietnam. It soon appears in the South as well.
April 7	In response to the NVA offensive, regular bombing of North Vietnam is resumed in Operation Linebacker.
April 16	B-52s bomb near Haiphong for the first time since 1968. Target restrictions are lifted from most areas.
April 17	The Soviets accuse U.S. aircraft of damaging four merchant ships in Haiphong Harbor.
April 29	The SA-7 (first used in the Middle East in 1969) downs its first plane in Vietnam.
April to September	Following a visit by the Soviet Air Force chief in late March, North Vietnam displays new air-defense techniques. These include multiple SA-2 site engagements, track-on-jam, optical tracking, and high-low engagements.
May 8	A-6s and A-7s from three carriers mine Haiphong and six other North Vietnamese ports, six years after Maxwell Taylor publicly proposed the move. Nixon offers to withdraw U.S. troops four months after a ceasefire.
May 10	In the single biggest day of air combat, navy Phantoms shoot down eight MiGs and the air force claims three. Cunningham and Driscoll of VF-96 bag three to emerge as the first ace crew of the war.
May 13	The air force destroys Thanh Hoa Bridge with laser-guided bombs.

June	North Vietnam introduces balloons with explosive charges.
	The U.S. ends its direct combat role in South Vietnam, leaving a residual force of sixty thousand personnel.
July	Grumman's new EA-6B Prowler is introduced to combat by VAQ-132, providing electronic monitoring and jamming support for air operations.
July 22	"Fat Albert," a black slow-moving SAM, is first noted.
August	U.S. warships shell Haiphong harbor.
September 11	The new "Fat Black" SAM, apparently invulnerable to ECM and standoff jamming, downs a Marine Corps F-4J. The VMF-333 team of Lasseter and Cummings makes the Marines' only MiG kill.
October 24	A seven-day bombing halt above the 20th Parallel goes into effect as a peace gesture. Bombing of supply routes south of the line continues at near-record levels.
December 4	North Vietnamese negotiators in Paris remain dilatory, despite Henry Kissinger's announcement two months earlier of a "breakthrough" in the peace talks.
December 14	President Nixon threatens renewed bombing if serious negotiations are not resumed within seventy-two hours.
December 18 through 29	Operation Linebacker II is launched with intense bombing of North Vietnam, including heavy B-52 operations. Minefields in Haiphong harbor and elsewhere are restocked.
December 25	A thirty-six hour bombing pause begins.
December 27	The Marine Corps logs its last fixed-wing aircraft combat loss.
December 30	Nixon orders another bombing halt as the North Vietnamese show interest in bargaining again.

1973

January 8	Kissinger and Le Duc Tho resume discussions in Paris.
January 9	U.S. fighters are allowed to pursue MiGs above the 20th Parallel.
January 12	Kovaleski and Wise of VF-161 off *Midway* score the last aerial kill of the war, the sixty-first for carrier aircraft.
January 15	Bombing, shelling, and mining of North Vietnam are halted as progress is reported in Paris.
January 27	An *Enterprise* F-4 flown by LCDR Harley Hall becomes the last Navy fixed-wing combat loss. Shot down near the DMZ, Hall disappears but his radar operator is rescued.
	A ceasefire agreement is signed in Paris, applicable to North and South Vietnam.
February 21	A ceasefire ensues in Laos.

1974

January	Fighting erupts again with two engagements between ARVN and communist forces. President Thieu reports thirteen thousand South Vietnamese troops and four thousand civilians killed in the year since signing of the ceasefire.
April	Communist insurgents tighten the ring around Phnom Penh, Cambodia.

1975

March	North Vietnamese forces begin their rapid final offensive, beginning near Ban Me Thuot in the central highlands.
April 17	Phnom Penh falls to communist forces.
April 29	The Marine Corps evacuates Americans from Saigon.
May 15	Marines land on Koh Tang Island to rescue the freighter *Mayaguez*, seized by Cambodian insurgents. American forces sustain sixty-eight casualties.

May 27   North Vietnamese and Viet Cong troops parade in Saigon.

August 23   The Pathet Lao forces consolidate the communist takeover in Laos. All of Vietnam, Laos, and Cambodia are under communist control, ending the Second Indochina War.

APPENDIX B

COMBAT SORTIES AND AIRCRAFT LOSSES

Fixed-Wing Combat Sorties

SOUTHEAST ASIA, April 1965–March 1973			NORTH VIETNAM, April 1965–March 1973		
USAF	1,766,000	(68%)	USN	275,000	(52%)
USN	510,000	(20%)	USAF	226,000	(43%)
USMC	320,000	(12%)	USMC	27,000	(5%)
	2,596,000			528,000	

**Fixed-Wing Aircraft Losses in
Southeast Asia**

January 1962–June 1973

	IN-FLIGHT			GROUND		
	Combat	Opera- tional	TOTAL	Combat	Opera- tional	TOTAL
USN	538	316	854	0	25	25
USMC	173	75	248	18	5	23
USAF	1,606	461	2,067	95	27	122
	2,317	852	3,169	113	57	170

Overall total: 3,339

Areas of In-Flight Battle Damage

	USN	USMC	USAF
North Vietnam	82%	17%	39%
South Vietnam	5%	71%	33%
Laos	11%	10%	25%
Other/Unknown	2%	2%	3%

Causes of In-Flight Fixed-Wing Losses

	USN	USMC	USAF
Antiaircraft Artillery	37%	14%	26%
Unknown	25%	33%	16%
Semiautomatic and Automatic	18%	50%	47%
Surface-to-Air Missile	15%	2%	7%
Own Ordnance	3%	?	1%
MiG Interceptors	2%	−1%	4%

(Excludes operational causes)

Navy Fixed-Wing In-Flight Combat Losses

	North Vietnam	South Vietnam	Laos	Other	TOTAL
A-1	36	4	6	2	48
A-4	172	4	16	3	195
A-6	38	1	10	2	51
A-7	39	3	13	0	55
F-4	64	4	6	1	75
F-8	54	3	1	0	58
Other*	41	8	6	1	56
	444	27	58	9	538

(*A-3 series, RA-5, RF-8, EA-1, OV-10, P-2, P-3, S-2)

Marine Fixed-Wing In-Flight Combat Losses

	North Vietnam	South Vietnam	Laos	Other	TOTAL
A-4/TA-4	7	51	4	0	62
A-6	10	4	1	1	16
F-4	7	47	11	0	65
F-8	2	7	1	0	10
Other*	3	15	0	2	20
	29	124	17	3	173

(*OV-10, EF-10, RF-4, KC-130, EA-6, O-1, TF-9)

Navy and Marine Corps
Aggregate Combat Losses in Flight

A-4/TA-4	257
F-4/RF-4	143
F-8/RF-8	88
A-6/EA-6	67
A-7	55
A-1/EA-1	49
RA-4	18
OV-10	13
KA-3/EA-3	6
EF-10	4
KC-130	3
P-2/OP-2	3
O-1	2
TF-9	1
P-3	1
S-2	1
	711

APPENDIX C

OVERALL AIR-TO-AIR COMBAT RESULTS

Enemy Aircraft Shot Down

	AN-2	MiG-17	MiG-19	MiG-21	TOTAL
USAF	0	61	8	68	137
USN/USMC	2	39	2	18	61
Air America*	2	0	0	0	2
	4	100	10	86	200

(*UH-1 helicopter)

Known U.S. Aircraft Lost to MiGs

Aircraft Type	USAF	USN-USMC	TOTAL
A-1E	1	0	1
A-1H	0	1	1
KA-3B	0	1	1
A-4C	0	1	1
RA-5C	0	1	1
A-6A	0	2	2
RC-47	1	0	1
F-4B/J	0	7	7
F-4C/D/E	35	0	35
F-8C/D/E	0	3	3
RF-101	1	0	1
F-102	1	0	1
F-105	21	0	21
	60	16	76

Summary of U.S. Losses

```
42  F-4s
21  F-105s
 3  F-8s
 2  A-1s
 2  A-6s
 1  A-4
 1  KA-3
 1  RA-5
 1  RC-47
 1  RF-101
 1  F-102
```
―――――――
76 lost to MiGs

Overall U.S. Exchange Ratio: 198–76, or 2.6–1

U.S. Exchange Rates,
Fighter Versus Fighter Only, 1965–73

U.S. Type	Air Force		USN-USMC	
F-4	107½-35	(3.07-1)	38.7	(5.42-1)
F-8			18-3	(6.00-1)
F-102	0-1	(0.00-1)		
F-105	27½-20	(1.37-1)		
	135-56	(2.41-1)	56-10	(5.60-1)

Enemy Types Shot Down
By U.S. Fighters Only

Enemy Type	Kills-Losses	Fighter Exchange Ratio
MiG-17	97-17	5.70-1
MiG-19	10-3	3.33-1
MiG-21	83-46	1.80-1
	190-66	2.86-1

Best U.S. Exchange Rates

USN F-8	6.00-1
USN F-4	5.42-1
USAF F-4	3.07-1
USAF F-105	1.37-1

Combined F-4 Exchange Rate: 145½-43, or 3.38-1

APPENDIX D

VIETNAM CARRIER DEPLOYMENTS
AUGUST 1964—JANUARY 1973

AIRCRAFT CARRIER	FLEET	VIETNAM DEPLOYMENTS		AIR WINGS EMBARKED
Hancock (CVA-19)	Pac	7 cruises*	1964-72	5 and 21
Oriskany (CVA-34)	Pac	7 cruises*	1965-73	16 and 19
Ranger (CVA-61)	Pac	7 cruises	1964-73	2, 9 and 14
Constellation (CVA-64)	Pac	6 cruises*	1964-73	9, 14 and 15
Coral Sea (CVA-43)	Pac	6 cruises*	1964-73	2 and 15
Bonhomme Richard (CVA-31)	Pac	6 cruises	1964-70	5, 19 and 21
Enterprise (CVAN-65)	Lant	6 cruises	1965-73	9 and 14
Kittyhawk (CVA-63)	Pac	6 cruises	1965-72	11
Ticonderoga (CVA-14)	Pac	5 cruises	1964-69	5, 16 and 19
America (CVA-66)	Lant	4 cruises	1968-73	6, 8 and 9
Midway (CVA-41)	Pac	3 cruises*	1965-73	2 and 5
Intrepid (CVS-11)	Lant	3 cruises	1966-69	10
Forrestal (CVA-59)	Lant	1 cruise	1967	17
Independence (CVA-62)	Lant	1 cruise	1969	7
F D. Roosevelt (CVA-42)	Lant	1 cruise	1966-67	1
Saratoga (CVA-60)	Lant	1 cruise	1972-73	3
Shangri-La (CVA-38)	Pac	1 cruise	1970	8

17 carriers		71 cruises		16 air wings
		*Plus 5 after January 1973		

Squadron Deployments by Aircraft Types
1964–1973

A-4 squadrons	107 cruises
F-4 squadrons	84 cruises
F-8 squadrons	57 cruises
A-7 squadrons	56 cruises
A-6 squadrons	33 cruises
RA-5 squadrons	31 cruises
A-1 squadrons	24 cruises
E-2 squadrons	24 cruises
A-3 squadrons	13 cruises*
EA-6 squadrons	3 cruises
	432 squadron cruises

*Includes EA-3, KA-3, and EKA-3

NOTES

1 BACKGROUND TO DOCTRINE

1. Norman Polmar, *Aricraft Carriers* (Garden City: Doubleday, 1969), p. 587.

2. Wynn Foster interview, Coronado, CA, November 1986.

3. James D. Ramage interview, Bonita, CA, February 1985.

4. *Navy and Marine Corps Air Operations, Korean Area 1950–1953*, Washington, D.C.: Office of Naval Aviation History. Hereafter cited as *Korean Area Summary*.

5. Ibid.

6. Barrett Tillman, "The Blue Blasters: History of VA-34," *The Hook* (Summer 1983).

2 RULES OF ENGAGEMENT

1. Curiously, LBJ also complained, "I can't ask American boys to go on fighting with one arm tied behind their backs." John Morrocco et al., *The Vietnam Experience: Thunder from Above* (Boston: Boston Publishing, 1984), p. 34.

2. Comment by W. A. Franke, commanding officer of VF-21, returned as POW in 1973.

3. For an extreme example of the effects of Soviet ships' anti-aircraft weapons, see Jack Broughton, *Thud Ridge* (New York: Lippincott, 1969).

4. James E. Fausz interview, Mesa, AZ, April 1984.

5. *The Vietnam Experience*, p. 56; amplified by naval aviators' comments, 1967-68.

6. Dave Richard Palmer, *Summons of the Trumpet* (New York: Ballantine Books, 1984), p. 163.

7. Vo Nguyen Giap interview, "Vietnam: A Television History" (Public Broadcasting System, 1983).

3   MORALE: THE ONLY WAR WE HAD

1. John B. Nichols diary entry, March 1968.

2. See James and Sybil Stockdale, *In Love and War* (New York: Harper & Row, 1984), which describes a personal account of POW–MIA families' efforts to deal with military and State Department representatives.

3. Barrett Tillman, "Are Navy Pilots Worth Saving?" *Soldier of Fortune* (April 1984).

4   THE SURFACE THREAT: AAA AND SAMS

1. *Korean Area Study* (Washington Navy Yard, Washington, D.C.: Office of Naval Aviation History).

2. Ibid.

3. Untitled study of U.S. air operations in Southeast Asia, 1964-73. Hereafter *Southeast Asia Statistical Summary* (Washington Navy Yard, Washington, D.C.: Office of Naval Aviation History).

4. Ibid.

5. Ibid.

6. William W. Momyer, *Airpower in Three Wars* (Washington, D.C.: Government Printing Office, 1978), p. 118.

7. *Southeast Asia Statistical Summary.*

8. John B. Nichols's cruise notes.

9. Momyer, *Airpower,* p. 136.

10. Robert B. Arnold, correspondence, April 1984.

5   THE AIRBORNE THREAT: MIGS

1. *Southeast Asia Statistical Summary.*

2. Momyer, *Airpower,* pp. 118-19.

3. *Southeast Asia Statistical Summary.*

4. Ibid.

5. Tape recording from USS *Coontz,* 9 July 1968.

6. "Tailhook '83." *The Hook* (Winter 1983).

6   ECM: THE ELECTRON WAR

1. *Location of Aircraft* reports, June 1965 and June 1967.

2. James E. Fausz interview; Mesa, AZ, March 1986.

3. Ibid.

4. Barrett Tillman, "After the Fight Was Over," *The Hook* (Summer 1984).

5. Curtis R. Dose interview, LaJolla, CA, November 1982.

7 STRIKE WARFARE, CV STYLE
    1. Robert B. Arnold, correspondence, April 1984.
    2. Jeff Earl, "The Real Man's Approach to Carrier Aviation," *The Hook* (Summer 1983).
    3. Robert B. Arnold, correspondence, April 1984.
    4. *Southeast Asia Statistical Summary*.
    5. David Anderton, *LTV A-7A/E* (Great Britain: Profile Publications, 1972).
    6. Polmar, *Aircraft Carriers*, p. 682.

8 PILOT DOWN: SEARCH AND RESCUE,
   ESCAPE AND EVASION
    1. D. G. Hartley, "Keeping Faith with Our People," *U.S. Naval Institute Proceedings* (February 1983).
    2. E. H. Tilford, Jr., *U.S. Air Force Search and Rescue in Southeast Asia* (Washington, D.C.: Government Printing Office, 1980).
    3. Ibid.
    4. Briefing by helicopter squadron HC-9, June 1982.
    5. *U.S. Navy In-Flight Aircraft Losses, SE Asia, 1964-73* (Washington, D.C.).
    6. Hartley, "Keeping Faith."
    7. Howard Rutledge, *In the Presence of Mine Enemies* (Boston: G. K. Hall, 1974).
    8. Hartley, "Keeping Faith."

9 WHAT IF?
    1. *History of VA-52, 1964-65*.
    2. Stanley Karnow, *Vietnam: A History* (New York: Viking, 1983), p. 415.
    3. Frank Futrell, *The USAF in Korea, 1950-1953* (New York: Duell-Sloane-Pearce, 1961), pp. 653-54.
    4. Malcolm Cagle and Frank Manson, *The Sea War in Korea* (Annapolis: Naval Institute Press, 1957), pp. 493-94.

GLOSSARY

AAA	antiaircraft artillery
ACM	air combat maneuvering
AEW	airborne early warning
AGL	above ground level
ARM	antiradiation missile
ARRS	Aerospace Rescue and Recovery Service
ASW	antisubmarine warfare
CAG	commander of a carrier air wing
CAP	combat air patrol
CarDiv	carrier division
CBU	cluster bomb unit
CCA	carrier-controlled approach
CNO	Chief of Naval Operations
CO	commanding officer
CVA	attack aircraft carrier
CTF	commander of task force
DMZ	Demilitarized Zone between North and South Vietnam
DOD	Department of Defense
ECM	electronic countermeasures
ECCM	electronic counter-countermeasures
EW	electronic warfare
FAC	forward air controller
GCI	ground-controlled intercept
HC	helicopter support squadron or aircraft
ICBM	intercontinental ballistic missile
ICC	International Control Commission
IR	infra-red; a heat-seeking or thermal-imaging device
MIA	missing in action
MiG	Soviet aircraft designed by Mikoyan and Gurevich
NAS	naval air station

NFO	naval flight officer; nonpilot aircrew member
NVAF	North Vietnamese Air Force
POL	petroleum-oil-lubricants
POW	prisoner of war
PRC	Peoples Republic of China
PT	patrol-torpedo boat
ROE	rules of engagement
RVAH	heavy reconnaissance aircraft or squadron
SAM	surface-to-air missile
SAR	search and rescue
TF	task force
VA	attack aircraft or squadron
VAQ	electronic warfare aircraft or squadron
VAW	early warning aircraft or squadron
VF	fighter aircraft or squadron
VFP	photographic aircraft or squadron

INDEX

213

THIS VIOLENT CENTURY

Bantam War Books Tell the Story of Military Conflicts Throughout the World

1918

April 21 Baron Manfred von Richthofen's career comes to an end. *A History of the Luftwaffe* by John Killen.

1919

Jan. 1 More than a thousand Soviet troops attack American soldiers entrenched around the village of Nijni Gora in northern Russia. *The Ignorant Armies* (April 1990).

1927

Oct. 18 HMS *L 4*, a British submarine under the command of Lt. Frederick J. C. Halahan, R.N., rescues the crew and passengers of the SS *Irene* from Chinese river pirates. *Submarine Warriors* by Edwyn Gray (July 1990).

Dec. 26   Chesty Puller drives off sandinista "bandits" who are attacking his train just outside El Sauce, Nicaragua. *Marine! The Life of Chesty Puller* by Burke Davis (February 1991).

April 10   German bombers attack the Spanish town of Guernica. It is the town's market day and 1,600 civilians die. *Full Circle* by Air Vice Marshal J. E. Johnson.

Aug. 17   Having missed their fighter escort, eleven out of twelve Japanese carrier-based attack bombers are shot down over Hangchow by defending Chinese fighter planes. *The Ragged, Rugged Warriors* by Martin Caidin.

Sept. 14   The author, a young British aviator, is called to active duty. It is going to be a very long war. *Tale of a Guinea Pig* by Geoffrey Page.

April 7   HMS *Sealion* in the middle of the German invasion fleet on its way to Norway watches the ships sail past. Rules of engagement prevent an attack. *Submarine Commander* by Ben Bryant.

May 10   The Phony War is over. German troops invade Belgium and Holland. *Churchill and His Generals* by Barrie Pitt.

Sept. 15   The critical day in the Battle of Britain. The

Luftwaffe is beaten back from her daylight skies and Stanford Tuck, one of Britain's greatest air aces, shoots down a German Me 100. *Fly for Your Life* by **Larry Forrester.**

Nov. 11 British Swordfish torpedo bombers attack the Italian fleet anchored in the harbor of Taranto. *To War in a String Bag* by **Charles Lamb.**

1941

March 15 A hunter killer group commanded by Captain Donald MacIntyre sinks a U-99 and captures its captain, submarine ace Otto Kretschmer. *U-Boat Killer* by **Donald MacIntyre.**

April 16 Egyptian liner *Zamzam* sunk in South Atlantic by German surface raiders. *The German Raider Atlantis,* by **Rogge and Frank.**

May 24 "I turned around to look for *Hood* and stared and stared and stared. It was clear to the horizon and *Hood* was no longer there. She'd had a crew of nearly fifteen hundred. Three of them survived." *Heart of Oak* by **Tristan Jones.**

May 27 German battleship *Bismarck* sunk. HMS *Hood* is avenged. *Pursuit* by **Ludovic Kennedy.**

July 4 The 10th Gurkhas with the 2nd Bn. of the 4th in reserve attack Vichy French and Syrian troops defending Deir-es-Zor, Syria. *The Road Past Mandalay* by **John Masters.**

Aug. 9 Douglas Bader loses a leg as his fighter plane is shot down over France. Fortunately it was one of his two artificial ones. *Reach for the Sky* by **Paul Brickhill.**

Oct. 31 U.S. destroyer *Rubin James* sunk by German submarine. *Tin Cans* by **Theodore Roscoe.**

Nov. 22 Major Robert Crisp fights his "Honey" tank against Rommel's panzers at Sidi-Rezegh in the North

African desert. *Brazen Chariots* by Donald Crisp.

Dec. 7   Japanese carrier-based aircraft attack the U.S. fleet at Pearl Harbor. *Day of Infamy* by Walter Lord.

Dec. 24   The gallant defenders of Wake Island are overwhelmed by a Japanese amphibious landing force. *The Story of Wake Island* by Brig. Gen. James P. S. Devereux.

Dec. 27   British and Norwegian commandos attack the German garrison at Vaagso, Norway. *The Vaagso Raid* by Joseph H. Devins, Jr.

1942

Jan. 27   Lt. Commander Joe Grenfiel, commanding USS *Gudgeon,* sinks the Japanese submarine *I-173* near Midway Island. *Combat Patrol* by Clay Bair, Jr.

Feb. 8   From the embattled fortress of Corregidor the submarine USS *Trout* loads two tons of gold bars and 18 tons of silver pesos for transport to Pearl Harbor. *Pig Boats* by Theodore Roscoe.

Feb. 11   Three German capital ships are making a run from the French port of Brest up the English Channel toward a safe haven in Germany. *Breakout!* by John Deane Potter.

March 6   Operation Nordpol commences with the capture of a British radio operator in Holland by Abwehr personnel. The problem now is to turn the agent so that he sends false messages to England. *London Calling North Pole* by H. J. Giskes.

May 8   British commandos blast their way into St. Nazaire harbor so as to destroy the Normandy dock. *The Greatest Raid of All* by C. E. Lucas Phillips.

June 1   Captain Frederic John Walker, R.N., in *Starling,* with *Wild Goose* and *Kite* in support as a hunter killer group stalk Captain Poser's *U-202*. This German submarine is hidden 800 feet below them in the depths of the Atlantic. ***Escort Commander*** by T. Robertson.

June 4 Nazi General Reinhard Heydrich dies of wounds received on May 27 when his car was bombed by Czech OSS agents. His side had neglected to develop penicillin. ***Seven Men at Daybreak*** by Alan Burgess.

June 16 Sub. Lt. C. L. Page captured and then executed by the Japanese. He'd stayed behind as a coastwatcher to radio intelligence reports on Japanese troop and naval movements from the Tabar Islands to Australia. ***The Coast Watchers*** by Eric A. Feldt.

June 21 Rommel captures the British North African fortress of Tobruk. ***With Rommel in the Desert*** by H. W. Schmidt.

June 27 Russian submarine *K-21* fires a spread of four torpedoes at the German battleship *Tirpitz*. ***Russian Submarines in Arctic Waters*** by I. Kolyshkin.

July 27 Special Air Service jeeps destroy Rommel's precious Ju 52 transport planes at Sidi Haneish airfield in North Africa. ***Stirling's Desert Raiders*** by Virginia Cowles.

Aug. 7 U.S. marines land on Guadalcanal. ***The Battle for Guadalcanal*** by Samuel B. Griffith II (November 1990).

Aug. 8 Wounded and nearly blind, Japanese ace Saburo Sakai nurses a shattered Zero fighter over five hundred miles of ocean after attacking the Americans on Guadalcanal. ***Samurai*** by Sakai and Roger Pineau.

Aug. 9 British bombers lay mines in the Channel to block the *Prince Eugen* from the Atlantic. ***Enemy Coast Ahead*** by Guy Gibson.

Aug. 15 The American tanker *Ohio* finally docks at

the besieged island of Malta in the Mediterranean. *Red Duster, White Ensign* by Ian Cameron.

Sept. 13   Over the North African desert, German ace Hans-Joachim, "The Star of Africa," with 158 victories, dies as he fails to successfully exit his burning Me 109. *Horrido!* by Raymond R. Toliver and Trevor J. Constable.

Sept. 17   Admiral Donetz secretly orders his U-boat commanders not to attempt to assist or reach the survivors of their attacks. *The Laconia Affair* by Leonce Peillard.

Oct. 4   British motor torpedo boats in battle action against German convoys off the Dutch coast. *Night Action* by Peter Dickens.

Dec. 11   British commandos who had paddled their fold-a-boats through sixty miles of German-occupied territory mine and sink several large German merchant ships tied up in the French harbor of Bordeaux. *Cockleshell Heroes* by Lucas-Phillips.

1943

Jan. 31   General Von Paulus surrenders the German 6th Army at Stalingrad. *Enemy at the Gates* by Walter Craig.

Feb. 7   Commander Howard W. Gilmore, wounded on the bridge of the USS *Growler,* gives the order, "Take her down." He does but his ship survives. *Sink 'Em All* by Charles A. Lockwood.

Feb. 26   British agent Yeo-Thomas, "The White Rabbit," parachutes behind German lines into occupied France. *The White Rabbit* by Bruce Marshall.

Feb. 28   Norwegian commandos sabotage the heavy-water plant at Vemork, Norway. *Assault in Norway* by Thomas Gallagher.

March 30   Upon landing in Norway, his unit is destroyed by the Germans and this Norwegian commando, Jan Baalsrud, embarks on an incredible journey of survival. *We Die Alone* by Horwith.

May 12   The German Afrika Korps in Tunisia surrenders. One unit, the 164th Light Afrika Division, fights on until the following day. *The Foxes of the Desert* by **Paul Carell.**

May 16   Lt. Machorton returns to Imphal from the jungles of Burma. Wounded, he had been left to die. *The Hundred Days of Lt. Machorton* by **Machorton and Henry Maule.**

May 17   Guy Gibson and Squadron 617 destroy the Moehne and Eder dams. *The Dam Busters* by **Paul Brickhill.**

May 30   Although American troops have secured the island of Attu in the Aleutians, individual Japanese defenders still lurk in the surrounding hills. *The Thousand Miles War* by **Brian Garfield (October 1990).**

July 8   Rudel's cannon-firing Stuka takes part in the biggest tank battle of World War II, Kursk, Russia. *Stuka Pilot* by **Hans Ulrich Rudel (November 1990).**

July 11   Allied troops invade Sicily. *One More Hill* by **Franklyn A. Johnson.**

July 11   General George Patton is very much there too. *War As I Knew It* by **George S. Patton.**

July 27   The German city of Hamburg is consumed by a firestorm. *The Night Hamburg Died* by **Martin Caidin (December 1990).**

Aug. 17   British bombers attack the German doomsday missile development base at Peenemünde. *V-2* by **Walter Dornberger.**

Sept. 9   Fresh from his triumphs in North Africa, Popski along with his jeeps is landed in Teranto harbor by the USS *Boise* so that his private army can commence its invasion of Italy. ***Popski's Private Army*** by Lt. Col. Peniakoff.

Sept. 12 Colonel Skorzeny rescues Mussolini. ***Commando Extraordinary*** by Charles Foley.

Sept. 14 Russ Carter parachutes into Paestum, which is just south of the Salerno beachhead. ***Those Devils in Baggy Pants*** by Russ Carter.

Oct. 11 Running on the surface in La Pérouse Strait, one of America's greatest submarines fails to survive an attack by Japanese aircraft. ***Wahoo: The Patrols of America's Most Famous World War II Submarine*** by Rear Admiral Richard H. O'Kane (Ret.).

Oct. 14 The Schweinfurt Ball Bearing works were the target. Sixty B-17s failed to return from it. ***Black Thursday*** by Martin Caidin.

Oct. 29 Three British POWs escape from Stalag-Luft III. ***The Wooden Horse*** by Eric Williams.

Nov. 2 American destroyers in battle action against the navy of Imperial Japan at the Battle of Empress Augusta Bay. ***Admiral Arleigh (31 Knot) Burke*** by Ken Jones and Hubert Kelley.

Nov. 5 Donald R. Burgett wins his paratrooper wings. ***As Eagles Screamed*** by Donald R. Burgett.

Nov. 13 The Japanese battleship *Hiei* goes to the bottom, sunk by marine and navy airmen. ***The Cactus Air Force*** by Thomas G. Miller, Jr.

Nov. 20 American marines land on the Japanese island of Tarawa. ***Tawara*** by Robert Sherrod.

Dec. 2 Bari, Italy. German bombers sink twenty Allied merchant ships, and a deadly, secret cargo is released. ***Disaster at Bari*** by Glen Infield.

1944

Jan. 3 "Pappy," after chalking up 25 victories gets shot down over Rabaul. *Baa, Baa, Black Sheep* by Gregory "Pappy" Boyington.

Feb. 1 American and Filipino guerrillas launch an offensive against the Japanese. *American Guerrilla in the Philippines* by Ira Wolfert.

Feb. 22 Heinz Knoke shoots down a B-17 Flying Fortress over his home town of Hameln, Germany. *I Flew for the Führer* by Heinz Knoke.

March 5 Brig. Tom Churchill takes command on the island of Vis in the Adriatic Sea. *Commando Force 133* by Bill Strutton.

March 18 Chindit units battle hand to hand with the Japanese invaders of Burma. *Fighting Mad* by "Mad" Mike Calvert.

March 20 USS *Angler* surfaces off Panay Island in the Japanese-occupied Philippines to rescue 58 refugees. *Guerrilla Submarines* by Ed Dissette.

April 13 Over Hamburg, Germany, an FW 190 becomes the author's 25th aerial victory. *Thunderbolt* by Robert S. Johnson, with Martin Caidin (September 1990).

June 6 In the first minutes of this day the green light goes on in a C-47 flying over the Cherbourg peninsula. *As Eagles Screamed* by Donald R. Burgett. *D-Day* by David Howarth.

June 9 Normandy beachhead. Keith Douglas KIA near Tilly-sur-Seulles. *Alamein to Zem Zem* by Keith Douglas.

June 22 An American pilot uses a 1,000-pound bomb to cure a long-standing rat problem in his old barracks now occupied by the Japanese. *Into the Teeth of the Tiger* by Donald S. Lopez.

June 24 Marine General "Howlin' Mad" Smith relieves Major General Ralph Smith from command of the 27th Infantry Division on the island of Saipan. *Coral* *and Brass* by General Holland "Howling Mad" Smith.

June 25 German ace Robert Spreckels shoots down British ace J.R.D. Braham in air combat over Denmark. *Night Fighter* by J.R.D. Braham.

June 26 The French port of Cherbourg falls to Allied invasion forces. *Invasion: They're Coming!* by Paul Carell.

June 29 An SS squadron in Russia on the Mogilev-Minsk road is shooting German officers found to be moving toward the rear without proper written orders. *The Black March* by Peter Neumann.

July 18 The city of St. Lô is finally secured. *The Clay Pigeons of St. Lô* by Grover S. Johns, Jr.

Aug. 15 Operation "Anvil," the allied landing in the South of France. "The best invasion I ever attended." *Up Front* by Bill Mauldin.

Sept. 15 A young marine goes ashore on Peleliu Island which was one of the most bitterly contested of the Pacific island landings. *Helmet for My Pillow* by Robert Leckie.

Sept. 17 Disguised as a slave laborer, British Sgt. Charles Coward, a prisoner of war in Germany, has just spent the night in hell, locked inside the Auschwitz concentration camp. He now knows the secret of the camp and has vowed to tell it to the world. *The Password Is Courage* by John Castle.

Oct. 3 A young infantry captain enters Germany. It is 11:15 A.M. and the war in Europe is a long way from being over. *Company Commander* by Charles Mac-Donald (August 1990).

Oct. 25 Lt. Seki successfully crashes his plane into the USS *St. Lô* (CVE-63) and sends this escort carrier to the bottom. *The Divine Wind* by Roger Pineau.

Having attacked a Japanese convoy with unbelievable

ferocity, *Tang* fires a final misfunctioning torpedo which turns back and sinks this famous submarine. *Clear the Bridge* by Richard O'Kane (November 1990).

Nov. 26 If you have ever wondered where some of our best writers are. Flying a P-51 on an escort mission over Hanover, Germany, Bert Stiles is KIA. *Serenade to the Big Bird.*

1945

Jan. 4 The 761st Tank Bn. attacks the town of Tillet. It is just to the west of Bastogne. *Hit Hard* by David J. Williams (May 1990).

Feb. 3 Convoy JW-64 sails north from England on its way to Russia. *A Bloody War, 1939-45* by Hal Lawrence.

Feb. 23 U.S. marines raise the American flag on the peak of Mt. Suribachi. *Iwo Jima* by Richard Newcomb.

Feb. 28 Company K attacks the town of Hardt just to the west of Düsseldorf, Germany. *The Men of Company "K"* by Leinbaugh and Campbell (November 1990).

March 15 Bob Clark, Clostermann's No. 4, flying a Hawker Tempest, shoots down an Me 262 piloted by Walter Nowotney, one of the Luftwaffe's greatest aces. *The Big Show* by Pierre Clostermann (November 1990).

April 1 The Japanese island of Okinawa is invaded. *Okinawa: Typhoon of Steel* by Belote and Belote.

April 16 A German steamship with 7,000 evacuees aboard is sunk outside of Hela, Prussia, by a Russian submarine. There are 170 survivors. *Defeat in the East* by J. Thorwald.

April 26 Adolph Galand leads a flight of Me 262 jet fighters in one of the last air battles of the European war. *The First and the Last* by Adolph Galand.

April 29 General Patton climbs down from one of his tanks to liberate the American POW camp of Mooseburg in Germany. *Prisoner of War* by Kenneth W. Simmons.

April 30 British "Crocodile" flame-throwing tanks take up positions outside the German town of Oldenburg. *Flame Thrower* by Andrew Wilson.

May 3 American armor overruns Jagvelband 44 at Salzburg-Maxglan, Germany, and the war is over for this squadron of futuristic German fighters. *Rocket Fighter* by Mano Ziegler.

May 8 German ace Erich Hartman chalks up his 352nd and final aerial victory. *Horrido!* by Raymond F. Toliver and Trevor J. Constable.

On a leave train bound for the South of France, the author learns that the war in Europe, at long last, is officially over. *To Hell and Back* by Audie Murphy.

June 2 The USS *Tinosa* recovers the crew of a ditched B-29 just south of the Japanese island of Kyushu. *Sink 'Em All* by Charles A. Lockwood.

June 21 The Japanese commander on Okinawa, General Ushijima, commits suicide. *Marine at War* by Russell Davis.

The U.S. high command declares Okinawa to be secured. *With the Old Breed* by Eugene B. Sledge (April 1991).

June 22 With her last two torpedoes, and just before heading home, USS *Crevalle* sinks a Japanese destroyer. *Hellcats of the Sea* by Lockwood and Adamson.

July 25 U.S. carrier aircraft raids Japan's Kure naval base, destroying or damaging most of what was left of the Imperial fleet. *Combat Command* by Frederick C. Sherman.

July 30 Japanese submarine *I-58* sinks the USS *Indianapolis*. *Abandon Ship!* by Richard E. Newcomb.

Aug. 17 A German U-boat commander surrenders to the Argentinian navy only to be accused of having brought Hitler to Antarctica. *U-Boat 977* by Heinz Schaeffer.

Sept. 2 General Wainwright, recently released from a Japanese POW camp, is present on the deck of the USS *Missouri* as the Japanese formally surrender. *General Wainwright's Story* by General Jonathan M. Wainwright. Edited by Robert Considine.

Sept. 11 After three and a half years of imprisonment, Australian soldiers and American sailors liberate the Kuching prison camp in North Borneo. *Three Came Home* by Agnes Newton Keith.

1950

June 25 The North Korean army moves south and the world is once more at war. *This Kind of War* by T. R. Fehrenbach (March 1991).

Dec. 10 Their breakthrough is now completed, and the marines who fought their way down from the Chosin Reservoir are finally in the clear. *The March to Glory* by Robert Leckie (June 1990).

1951

April 22 In the Battle of Solma-Ri, waves of Chinese infantry engulf the British Gloucester regiment. The survivors fight their way out to the south. *Now Thrives the Armourers* by Robert O. Holles.

1955

Jan. 4   On the Foum-Toub-Arris road four men are ambushed and burnt to death in their jeep by Algerian rebel forces. *The War in Algeria* by Pierre Leulliette.

1956

Oct. 10   Dedean Kimathi, the most wanted Mau Mau terrorist, is taken by four Kikuyu tribal policemen. *Manhunt in Kenya* by Sir Philip Goodhart and Ian Henderson.

1958

April 5   A 28-year-old police constable accepts the surrender of Hor Lung, the last of the top level Chinese Communist leaders at large in Malaya. *The War of the Running Dogs* by Noel Barber.

1963

June 11   A Buddhist monk burns himself to death on a street corner in Saigon. *The New Face of War* by Malcolm Browne.

1964

Nov. 24   Belgian Paras and the Lima One Flying Column of mercenaries save the lives of a thousand hostages in the Congo. *Save the Hostages* by David Reed.

1965

May 15   *SR-71*, the legendary recon U.S. aircraft, sets an 80,000-foot Mach 3.12 record. Twenty-five years later the *New York Times*, on February 24, 1990, reports that the air force will retire it. *Air War Vietnam* by Frank Harvey.

June 17 Navy Phantoms shoot down the first MiGs to be destroyed over Vietnam. *The Story of Air Fighting* by J. E. Johnson.

Dec. 18 Air cavalrymen are going into a hot landing zone at Ben Khe, Vietnam. *Year of the Horse—Vietnam* by Col. Kenneth D. Mertel.

1966

Jan. 17 A B-52 collides with its KC-135 tanker and a hydrogen bomb is lost. *One of Our H-Bombs Is Missing!* by Flora Lewis.

Oct. 13 A navy flyer's wife receives a telegram listing her husband as MIA. His plane was seen to explode over enemy-occupied territory. No parachute was observed and no radio distress calls were received. *Touring Nam* by Greenburg and Norton.

1967

Sept. 15 The Brown Water Navy's Force 117 goes into battle along the Rach Ba Rai against the 263rd Vietcong Main Force Bn. *Seven Firefights in Vietnam* by John A. Cash, John Albright, and Allan W. Sandstrum.

1968

Jan. 29 The Tet offensive starts and a marine doctor has no clue as to what the next two days will bring. *12, 20 & 5, a Doctor's Year in Vietnam* by John A. Parrish, M.D.

Feb. 25 Khe Sanh. A marine patrol is ambushed. One third of it returns to the perimeter. *Welcome to Vietnam, Macho Man* by Ernest Spencer.

July 3 A long year starts for an American soldier who has just landed in Vietnam. *One Soldier* by John Shook.

Nov. 15 Near Binh Tri village a scout dog finds a Vietcong mine. Casualties: dead 1 dog, 1 PRU, 12 others wounded. *The Advisor* by John L. Cook.

1970

Oct. 10 There is a patrol just outside the village of Truong Lam, and the word is "Incoming!" *Platoon Leader* by James R. McDonough.

1972

April 1 An EB-66 meets a SAM 2 just south of the DMZ and the co-pilot punches out at 30,000 feet. *Bat-21* by William C. Anderson (January 1991).

The Ultimate Novel of Air Combat

WARRIORS
by
BARRETT TILLMAN

"The most intelligent thriller I've seen this year."
-- Tom Clancy

Commander John Bennett values flesh-and-blood fighter pilots over high technology -- and he gets a chance to put his theories to the test. Invited by the Saudi king to build a secret air wing capable of matching the Israeli air force, Bennett recruits American and British top guns to train a corps of young Saudi pilots -- the "Tiger Force." It's a strategist's dream come true: a once-in-a-lifetime opportunity to launch Bennett's brand of young warriors into military history. But now, as a fierce Arab-Israeli war breaks out, thundering confrontations high above the desert will determine the fate of nations -- and give John Bennett's Tigers the fight of their lives.

"Today's fighter pilots are the last true warriors extant in our uncertain age. Tillman captures their honor, skill, and courage perfectly in this excellent book." -- Stephen Coonts, bestselling author of *Flight of the Intruder*.

WARRIORS. On sale now wherever Bantam Falcon Books are sold.

Join the Allies on the Road to Victory
BANTAM WAR BOOKS

"This is a story of one uncommon man's adventures, daring, honesty, and dedicated service to his country.... There will never be another like him." -- Barry Goldwater

I COULD NEVER BE SO LUCKY AGAIN
AN AUTOBIOGRAPHY
BY GENERAL JAMES H. JIMMY DOOLITTLE
WITH CARROLL V. GLINES

Pilot, scholar, daredevil, general...James "Jimmy" Doolittle is one of America's greatest heroes. In a life filled with adventure and achievement, Doolittle did it all. As a stunt pilot, he thrilled the world with his aerial acrobatics. As a scientist, he pioneered the development of modern aviation technology. During World War II, he served his country as a fearless and innovative air warrior, organizing and leading the devastating raid against Japan immortalized in the film Thirty Seconds Over Tokyo. Now, for the first time, here is his life story -- modest, revealing, and candid as only Doolittle himself can tell it.

I COULD NEVER BE SO LUCKY AGAIN is the story of the successes and adventures, the triumphs and tragedies of a true American hero -- a far-seeing leader whose courage, devotion, and daring changed the course of modern history...and continues to make its influence felt to this day.

On sale in hardcover wherever Bantam Books are sold.

AN340 -- 10/91

THE STORY OF AN AMERICAN HERO

☐ YEAGER: An Autobiography   25674-2/$5.95

The story of Chuck Yeager who rose from rural boyhood to become the one man who, more than any other, led America into space. From his humble West Virginia roots to his adventures as a World War II fighter pilot; from the man who escaped from German-occupied France to the test pilot who first broke the sound barrier: this is the real story of the man with the RIGHT STUFF.

☐ YEAGER: AN AUTOBIOGRAPHY is now on
     audiocassette!   45012-3/$7.95

This exclusive 60-minute audio adaptation of the bestselling autobiography, YEAGER: AN AUTOBIOGRAPHY, features General Chuck Yeager telling in his own words the amazing story of his life and exploits.

☐ PRESS ON! Further Adventures in the Good Life
     by Chuck Yeager   28216-6/$4.95

PRESS ON! is a remarkable portrait of a remarkable individual—it completely captures Yeager's head-on approach to living the good life. Using extensive examples and stories from all the times of his life, Chuck Yeager makes it clear that he always did—and always will—live the way he wants to.